BEGINNER'S GUIDE TO
REPAIRING LIONEL® TRAINS

Ray L. Plummer

KALMBACH BOOKS

Copyright © 1998 by Kalmbach Publishing Co. All rights reserved. This book may not be reproduced in part or in whole without written permission of the publisher, except in the case of brief quotations used in reviews. Published by Kalmbach Publishing Co., 21027 Crossroads Circle, Waukesha, WI 53187.

Printed in the United States of America

97 98 99 00 01 02 03 04 05   9 8 7 6 5 4 3 2 1

For more information, visit our website at http://www.kalmbach.com

Publisher's Cataloging in Publication
(Provided by Quality Books, Inc.)

Plummer, Ray L.
    Beginner's guide to repairing Lionel trains / Ray
L. Plummer.
  —1st ed.
    p. cm.
    ISBN: 0-89778-438-3

    1. Railroads—Trains—Models—Repairing.
2. Lionel Corporation. I. Title.

TF197.G73 1997   625.1'9
                           QBI97-40700

Book Design: Sabine Beaupré
Cover Design: Kristi Ludwig

Lionel® is the registered trademark of Lionel Corporation, Chesterfield, Michigan. This book is neither authorized nor approved by Lionel Corporation.

CONTENTS

Introduction 5

I. Getting That Old Train Running Again
    One: Opening the Box 7
    Two: Understanding the Transformer 9
    Three: Setting Up the Track 13
    Four: Servicing the Locomotive 20
    Five: Preparing the Cars 26
    Six: Setting Up the Accessories 31

II. Track Layout and Wiring
    Seven: Basic Layout Design and Construction 35
    Eight: Basic Layout Wiring 48

III. Classic Toy Train Technology
    Nine: Basic Mechanics for Toy Train Tinkerers 58
    Ten: Electrical Components Before the Electronic Age 67

Afterword 78

INTRODUCTION

So, you found that old electric train in the attic—the one you played with when you were a kid. Or maybe it was your father's or your grandfather's set. Perhaps you picked up a box with a locomotive, some cars, track, and a transformer at a rummage sale or swap meet, and now you're wondering how to get the thing running again.

You're in luck!

Most vintage toy trains were built to last. Unlike so many toys today, they were designed to endure long use and rough handling by children and keep right on working, with only the simplest, most basic care and maintenance. As a result, electric trains of any age usually can be awakened from hibernation quite easily, provided they were not severely damaged by their original owners and were stored in a friendly environment, away from dampness and extreme temperature.

This book will show you how to revive that cherished train, step by step. Beginning with putting the track together and hooking up the transformer correctly and then getting the train to run and the accessories to operate as intended, it can help you achieve maximum enjoyment from some of the finest toys of all time.

This book will also help you add to your basic set until, if you are so inclined, you eventually build it into a functioning model railroad layout. Or, if you are more the collector type and would like to acquire examples of toy trains from different eras or manufacturers, you'll find the information necessary to help you get your collectibles into shape before putting them on display.

Best of all, this book doesn't require any advance knowledge on your part. You don't need special skills or equipment to perform primary-level maintenance and repair on trains made before computer chips, can motors, and circuit boards came into common use in the 1980s. These toys were designed so that a twelve-year-old could understand how to set them up and keep them running by using common sense and making sure he cleaned and lubricated them on a regular basis. Believing that anyone reading this far has the ability and desire to do what that mythical preadolescent could do, I've explained what to do and how to do it in simple, straightforward language.

Section I features chapters organized so that what you generally need to know in order to get your train up and operating initially is at the beginning. Then I provide additional information.

Specifics and examples are handled in greater depth and detail.

Section II contains some time-honored layout designs that provide for interesting operation and imitate real railroad practice within limited space. Basic wiring diagrams and control systems for larger layouts are also covered.

Section III concentrates on the fundamental mechanical and electrical principles underlying classic toy train technology. Those concepts are examined theoretically in isolation and then combined to form sophisticated repair and tinkering projects. For those of you who want to learn to do more, I close by recommending some other Greenberg and Kalmbach books that deal with advanced layouts and repair techniques. In other words, your education in this hobby is just beginning.

Just how far you venture into handling your train repairs and resuscitations is your decision. All the same, don't be frightened away by the technical aspects, and never underestimate your capacity to master them. Almost anyone can. A tremendous amount of pride in accomplishment, not to mention plenty of downright fun, comes along when you enter this dimension of the hobby. Expect your patience and self-confidence to grow, along with the level of your satisfaction, as you acquire new knowledge, skills, and experiences while exploring the inner workings of your trains.

How can I be so sure about what you'll feel? I've been all around the pike during my half-century in this hobby, from running trains on the living room floor to building elaborate model railroads and displaying several collections on the walls. All of these endeavors were satisfying in their time, but my interests inevitably changed. However, the one activity I enjoyed the most over the years was bringing trains back to life, making weary old ones look and run like new again. Maybe that's a function of my advancing age. Perhaps I'm subconsciously looking for someone to do that to me.

We're ready to go, except that I first want to thank a few people at Kalmbach Publishing Co. for helping me put this book together. My friend Dick Christianson suggested that I share a little of what I've learned from half a century of repairing and restoring Lionel trains. Then Roger Carp came up with some ideas about what to write and how to arrange the chapters. He edited my manuscript, and Ann Sargent served as copy editor. Kristi Ludwig created the cover, Sabine Beaupré designed the book, and Rick Johnson took care of the illustrations. As always, Bill Zuback and his excellent staff handled the photographs, and Julie LaFountain performed an amazing assortment of other editorial tasks with ease. Enough of this. Let's get started.

I. GETTING THAT OLD TRAIN RUNNING AGAIN

Chapter One

OPENING THE BOX

"Old Electric Train"—that's what it says on the cardboard box. Can all of it be in there? It seems so much smaller than you remember. The anticipation in the air jacks up the atmospheric pressure by at least three millibars.

Perhaps the excitement stems from having the corrugated carton in which the train was originally shipped: from Lionel at Irvington, American Flyer at New Haven, Marx at Girard, or Ives at Bridgeport. After all, boxed sets are highly prized today. Even if you're not that fortunate, and your newly discovered treasure chest once contained canned beans or laundry detergent, it doesn't matter. The thrills triggered by the presence of the train are the same—like Christmas and your birthday wrapped up together.

Open the box carefully. Take a running inventory as you unpack. Although train sets varied widely in their components and consists, certain essentials were common to all of them:

• Obviously, there should be a locomotive—usually of steam, diesel, or electric profile. There should also be some freight or passenger cars for it to pull—three or four of these in most instances.

• Enough sections of track to form a small layout came with the basic train. Most people bought additional pieces for expansion. Whether your set is O or O27 gauge, you'll need at least eight curved track sections to assemble a circle in order to test-run your train.

• There must also be a transformer, a little box (usually black) to be connected between the electrical outlet on the wall and the track. Its function is to reduce the 115-volt house current to a safer level—somewhere between 5 and 20 volts—so that the trains can be handled without the danger of a severe electric shock. The transformer regulates the speed of the train, controls its direction, and activates the whistle or horn on models that are so equipped.

You may run across a box of old electric trains in your attic or basement, or you may buy one at a rummage sale or train meet. Courtesy *Classic Toy Trains* magazine.

• You will also need a connector, commonly known as a "lockon." This little device snaps onto the track and holds the lead wires from the transformer in place. Two short pieces of wire are required between the transformer and the lockon. Look for them in the bottom of the box.

These basic set components are needed to run the train. There also may be special track sections for uncoupling the train and activating the onboard mechanisms of operating cars. Track switches to change the train's route are common additions. You may even discover toy train accessories of any number of types and configurations in the box. These things were popular. Many were merely decorative pieces to add "real railroad" atmosphere to the layout. Some lit up; others provided movement or sound while appearing to serve some useful or civic function in Toy Train Town. We'll get to them later.

There usually is at least one baffling item in every box of trains. My best advice is to disregard it. If the item is important (maybe it's a missing part), that will become apparent as you go along.

Lionel included a locomotive, rolling stock, and track with all its sets, regardless of whether they were intended for the low-end O27 market (left) or the high-end O gauge (above). All catalog illustrations and instruction sheets courtesy Lionel Corporation.

Chances are, this oddball piece was lying near the track when someone last put away the train.

Now that you've unpacked the box and taken a quick inventory of its contents, you should conduct a visual inspection of the individual items. Examine each piece carefully, inside and out, to determine whether there are any bent, broken, loose, or missing parts that might get in the way of a mechanical function on the toy railroad. Although unsightly, damaged external trim parts may be ignored for now. Check for signs of deterioration that may have occurred during storage.

Rust is the biggest problem with trains that have been packed away in damp basements. It is readily apparent on the exposed metal surfaces, such as car wheels and track. Visible external rust usually indicates the likelihood of internal rust as well. It may be inside the locomotive mechanism or the transformer case. Finding heavy rust on anything in the train box should be taken as a sign of potentially serious trouble.

Remove loose dust and dirt from the exterior surfaces of your train with a clean, dry paintbrush. If necessary, follow up with Pledge or WD-40 on a soft cloth.

Of course, trains stored in hot attics can have their own set of problems. For example, many plastic parts, even entire car bodies, tend to warp and disfigure when they get too hot. This condition is usually quite obvious. Repeated overheating while in storage can also cause the insulation around wires to dry out, crack, and break. When this happens to a locomotive or operating car, it can be very annoying. However, when the line cord and plug of a transformer are involved, it can be downright dangerous. Therefore, check all exposed wires for cracks and bare spots. Wiggle and bend each one to be sure that the insulation is still intact and supple. You really can't be too careful here.

Next, spin the locomotive wheels by hand to see that they turn freely without binding. Check to see whether anything inside the mechanism has become loose or stuck; it could cause a short circuit or other trouble when you apply track power. Spin the car wheels, too, and inspect them for binding and scraping or bent axles.

This is also a good time to do some preliminary cleaning of the exterior surfaces of the locomotive and cars. Use a clean, dry paintbrush to remove superficial dirt and dust. This gets into all the cracks and corners very well. If the trains still appear dingy, gently applying a little Pledge or another mild furniture polish on a soft cloth usually works wonders. Light rubbing is the key. Some people prefer to use a petroleum-based preparation, such as WD-40 or CRC 5-56. You'll find that basically it's a matter of personal taste and choice. Heavier cleaning jobs require different products, as I'll explain in a later chapter.

Chapter Two

UNDERSTANDING THE TRANSFORMER

Although it may be old, your toy train transformer should give you no trouble, provided you use it correctly and keep it in good condition. Be aware, however, that your transformer operates on 115 volts of electricity, the same as a power tool or household appliance, so you should develop a cautious attitude toward it.

Any transformer, regardless of its size, can be potentially dangerous if misused or mishandled. So:
- Use care when plugging it in and unplugging it. Grasp the plug itself; never pull on the cord.
- Don't use your transformer if you or it are wet.
- Never leave it plugged in when not in use.
- Hook up your transformer only as directed.
- Don't use it for any purpose other than powering toy trains.
- Never overload it beyond capacity by attempting to power too many trains or accessories.
- Unplug your transformer if it gets hot.
- Never impede the air circulation around or underneath it.
- Don't take your transformer apart; instead, leave that to a qualified service technician.

Transformer Inspection and Testing

Before you do anything with your transformer, check it over carefully. Start by looking for visible signs of scorching, discoloration, or disfigurement on the transformer case. This usually indicates that the unit was severely overheated at some point and probably shouldn't be trusted. My best advice is to throw it away and get a new one.

Next, make sure the plug and line cord are firmly attached. Determine that the insulation on the cord is intact, with no bare spots or cracks showing. Bend and twist the cord; it should be supple and not stiff.

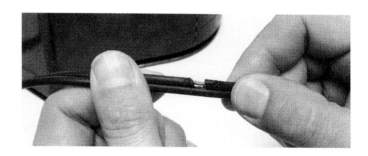

Carefully check the insulation on the transformer cord for signs of deterioration. This one has bare wire showing and should be replaced before the unit is plugged in.

Then check to see that all the binding post terminals, or studs, are tightly seated. Each of the handles, levers, and knobs should move freely, without sticking or binding. The buttons should spring back when you release them.

If your transformer passes this preliminary inspection, go ahead and plug it in. You should hear a slight audible hum or buzz; that's normal. Let the transformer run for an hour. At that time, it should be mildly warm to the touch but not hot.

Now attach a wire to one of the binding post terminals and turn the throttle to the "off" position. Carefully touch the other end of the wire to the second binding post terminal. Nothing should happen. Then turn the throttle about halfway up and touch the wire to the second terminal again. If you see a spark, the transformer is working.

If your transformer flunks *any* of these inspections or tests, turn it over to a qualified technician for service or replace it. Taking the transformer apart for any reason is not recommended because of the potential shock or fire hazard if you touch something wrong or don't get it back together right.

To test your transformer, attach a wire to one of the binding post terminals. Then, with the throttle halfway up, carefully touch the other end of the wire to a second terminal. If you see a spark, the transformer is working.

A schematic diagram showing how a transformer reduces 115-volt electrical current into fixed and variable low voltages that are suitable for operating toy trains.

What a Transformer Does

Most electric power utilities in the United States supply 115 volts of 60-cycle alternating current (AC) to their residential customers. This is the standard service, which is efficient and economical for family use. However, this household voltage is high enough to cause severe electric shock under certain circumstances.

Since children are not always careful, and the tracks upon which electric trains run are essentially "bare wires," toy train producers design their motors to work on much lower voltage. That's where transformers come in: Their main function is to reduce the 115-volt house power to a relatively harmless maximum of about 20 volts to power an electric train. Although the voltage may be stepped down, the alternating nature and 60-cycle frequency of the current remain unchanged.

How fast a toy train moves is determined by a rheostat, which is built into the transformer and usually attached to an external lever, handle, or knob. A rheostat serves as a throttle by varying the amount of voltage that is fed into the track, normally in a range of 5 to 20 volts. Many transformers also have provisions for supplying continuous specific fixed voltages to power accessories.

The reversing control found on most transformers is a button, lever, or switch that momentarily interrupts the flow of power to the track, thereby tripping the sequence reverse mechanism installed in the locomotive. The same effect can be obtained by turning the throttle down to zero and back up again.

Whistle control circuits are found in all but the smallest Lionel transformers. When activated, they send a surge of direct current (DC) voltage through the track to trigger the whistle or horn relay in the train. At the same time, the regular alternating current track power is boosted slightly to compensate for the drain caused by the whistle motor kicking in.

Types of Transformers

Lionel and other toy train manufacturers made transformers in huge quantities and in a variety of types and styles. These devices were designed to do essentially the same thing, which is why the brands were considered to be virtually interchangeable. But the transformers offered by The A. C. Gilbert Co. and Louis Marx & Co. had slightly lower output voltages, which resulted in a slower maximum train speed. This was noticeable when they were used to run the larger Lionel locomotives.

Transformers have traditionally been classified according to their wattage ratings, which range all the way from 25 to 350. The wattage rating is a measure of the maximum amount of electricity a transformer can draw from the household power lines without overheating. More simply and practically put, it is an indication of a transformer's capacity to run trains, handle accessories, and illuminate light bulbs at the same time. Generally, bigger is better. The higher a transformer's wattage rating, the more you can efficiently operate with it.

Lionel advised customers to buy a transformer that was large enough to provide for future expansion. It published guidelines that included the wattage requirements for some of its products. Although motivated by the desire to sell more transformers, these ideas were fairly realistic:

Basic O Gauge Locomotive	20–25 watts
With Whistle, add 10 watts	30–35 watts
With Smoke, add 5 more watts	35–40 watts
Automatic Accessories	12–15 watts
Operating Accessories	10–25 watts
Twelve-volt Lamps (each)	2–3 watts
Eighteen-volt Lamps (each)	5 watts

The wattage requirements added up quickly, particularly if an outfit came with illuminated cars and an operator planned to use automatic track switches with illuminated lanterns and controllers, not to mention a few accessories with lamps in them. Other variables included the size of the track layout and the number of cars in the train. Operating cars and accessories that weren't activated while the train was moving did not have to be counted. Still, it's easy to understand why transformers rated at 100 or more watts were so popular with those who wanted more than a loop around their Christmas tree.

During the 1970s, when consumer protection assumed greater importance, the federal government banned the manufacture of high-wattage transformers intended for use as children's toys. Although Uncle Sam's technical language was different, the law, which is still on the books, effectively outlawed traditional transformers that were rated at more than 90 watts.

So, if the layout you're planning needs more power than that, you have four options: 1) write your congressman to change the law; 2) take out a second mortgage on your house so you can afford to buy one of the new electronic control systems as an alternate power source; 3) take a lower mortgage, but a higher risk, and get a secondhand high-wattage transformer from the old days; or 4) turn to Chapter 8 to find out how you can hitch up a team of smaller transformers to perform the work of a larger one on your layout.

Because so many of the big transformers are still alive and capable of service in spite of their vintages, I'll treat their use in depth. However, one final word of caution: If you're fortunate enough to own one of these powerhouses, handle it with the care and respect that it demands.

Another way of classifying transformers is according to the number of throttle rheostats and/or binding post terminals on them. There is great variety among the models. I've long thought that Lionel went overboard with the number of binding posts and the combinations of fixed voltages available, often to the confusion of everyone. But nobody could say its transformers weren't sophisticated and versatile.

Small transformers (i.e., under 150 watts) and a few of the larger ones have only one throttle and are intended to run only one train and a complement of accessories.

Single-throttle models with two binding posts are easy to classify: two binding posts mean two wires to the track. It doesn't matter which one goes to which.

Transformers with three binding-post terminals usually provide two different variable track-voltage ranges, controlled by the same throttle.

Models with four or more terminals and only one throttle offer different variable track-voltage ranges, along with fixed voltages to power accessories. These voltage values usually are indicated on the nameplate or the case of a transformer.

Large transformers (i.e., 150 or more watts) customarily have more than one throttle. For example, the Lionel model KW features two throttles, and

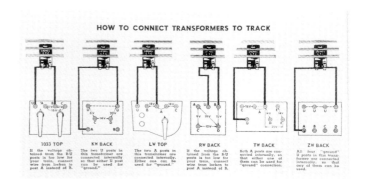

Basic variable-voltage track connections using several popular Lionel transformers.

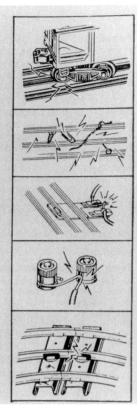

Check These Trouble Spots

A derailed car truck. If trouble persists remove all cars and locomotive from the track. Then look for:

Nails, screws, tinsel, etc. across the track. Sometimes a "magnetraction" locomotive will pick up a small iron object and hold it to the track from underneath.

Long wire ends connected to the two lockon clips touching each other.

A bare wire touching two binding posts of a transformer or an accessory piece of equipment.

Broken or displaced insulation between center rail and track tie. This may sometimes be difficult to find. If necessary check each track section separately.

Common causes of short circuits.

the top-of-the-line ZW has four. These independent throttle controls each have their own set of variable- and fixed-voltage terminals and can be hooked up as though they are separate transformers. When using a ZW, you can achieve fixed voltages by setting one or more of the throttles in advance.

Circuit Breakers

The main safety consideration in a transformer is a working circuit breaker. Toy railroads have always been prone to accidental short circuits from derailed rolling stock, stray tinsel, metallic toys, and other objects that somehow land on the track.

In simple terms, a "short circuit" is a condition in which the electric current from the center rail bypasses the motor that it's supposed to operate and flows instead into one of the outside running rails and back to the transformer. When this happens, the train stops, the lights dim or go out, and the transformer overheats. If the transformer is unprotected by a circuit breaker, it will burn out or up!

For this reason, toy train manufacturers installed circuit breakers in many, though not all transformers. They didn't equip some of their small "economy" units with circuit breakers despite the fact that those transformers might have carried the "UL" approval label. (Don't ask me how that happened!)

There are two basic types of circuit breakers in common use:

• Type A has a very positive action. When it senses overheating in the circuit, a spring-loaded breaker pops open. It has to be reset manually each time. Resetting devices can be found in the old "outboard" circuit breakers, which were marketed as "accessories" by Lionel, Gilbert, and Marx. They also appear built into some Gilbert and Marx transformers.

• Type B is by far the more common type of circuit breaker. It, too, is a thermal device, though one that works automatically. Sensing the short circuit a few seconds after it occurs, the breaker opens. The breaker then closes automatically, but it will reopen immediately if the short circuit still exists. This sequence continues until the short is corrected. Type B breakers are found in all Lionel and most of the later Gilbert transformers. Some even have blinking red lights connected to them.

Most of the Lionel transformers produced since World War II that have a rating of at least 45 watts come with built-in circuit breakers. Among those Lionel models that did not are the 1011, 1012, 1014, 1015, and 1016; there probably are others.

Similarly, most of the transformers Gilbert made for its American Flyer line with a rating of 40 watts or higher feature circuit breakers. Exceptions exist, but they aren't well documented. I once found a 75-watt unit without a breaker in it. Maybe it was a production error. Maybe not! The only Marx transformers that have circuit breakers are the ones with an obvious reset button on them.

Using a transformer with a working circuit breaker is a top priority for operating your trains safely. When in doubt about a model, I recommend having a professional check it.

A service technician can check a transformer and adjust your breaker, if necessary, in a few minutes. The alternative could be a smoky disaster. The only good place for an unprotected transformer is in a landfill.

Chapter Three
SETTING UP THE TRACK

While there is much to be said for starting out with brand new track, used sections that are clean and in good condition can be quite serviceable. They usually cost less than new track, though they may require a little preparation.

Begin by inspecting each section to make sure the pins are tight, rail openings are clean, and third-rail insulators are in place. Sight along the rails to see that they aren't bent, kinked, or squashed. If you can't satisfactorily straighten a section by hand, throw it away. The same goes for badly rusted pieces.

Next, scour the running surfaces of the rails with a Scotch-Brite pad to assure good electrical contact with the train. Never use steel wool for this, because any metallic residue left on the rails will be picked up by your locomotive's Magne-Traction and end up damaging the mechanism.

If your track is exceptionally dirty, you ought to consider washing it at this point in a strong solution of laundry detergent and water. Any kind of detergent you have on hand will do. (I usually use the bulk stuff at 30 cents per pound; my shirts and socks have never complained.) After putting

Use needlenose pliers on the web of the rail, as shown, to slightly reduce the diameter of each of the rail openings and thereby obtain a snug fit.

the track in the solution, scrub each section with a stiff brush. Then rinse it under warm running water and air-dry it thoroughly.

Tighten any loose pins by squeezing the web of the rail with a pair of needlenose pliers. Use the same technique on the openings at the other end to assure a snug fit when you join the sections.

Putting Together a Test Track

The process of assembling track sections into a layout hasn't changed. It doesn't matter whether you use sections with an O or O27 gauge profile in their original sharp turning radii or prefer any of the new, wider curvatures now on the market.

Join two sections by grasping them firmly and inserting the pins into the holes. Be careful not to bend the running rails by squeezing them together too much. A slight rocking and rolling motion sometimes helps, particularly with new track. The

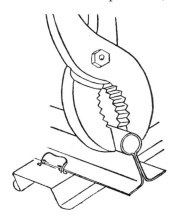

Be sure you tighten the openings of each rail so the sections of track can't work themselves apart.

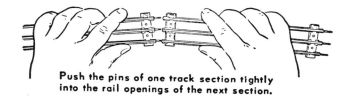

Push the pins of one track section tightly into the rail openings of the next section.

Joining sections of track is easy to do.

13

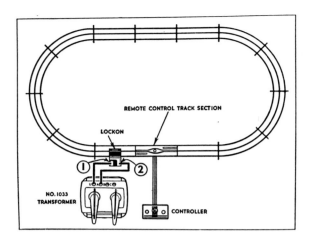

A simple oval of three-rail track is all you need to test an electric train.

Attach the lockon as shown here. Be sure it snaps in place under the center and outer rails.

goal is to get the sections to mate snugly. Push the pins in as far as you can by hand; relying on tools for this task can distort the rails or ties.

You don't need a large oval of track to test-run your train. Eight curved and four or six straight sections should be plenty. If you have a Remote Control Section for uncoupling and unloading, use it as part of the layout.

After you've assembled the track into an oval, attach a lockon between the center rail and one of the outer running rails on any straight section. You'll recall from the first chapter that a lockon is used to connect wires from the transformer to the track. Next, using a knife or a wire-stripping tool, remove the insulated covering from both ends of two short pieces of connecting wire. If you don't

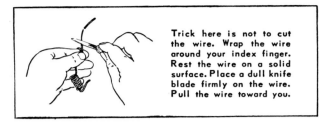

Strip the insulation from the connecting wires.

have any of the wire that originally came with the train, try using hookup ("doorbell") wire, which is available from hardware and electronics supply stores. I find that 18- or 20-gauge wire works best.

On the lockon, push down the upper half of the wire clip until the metal loop in the lower part projects through the slot in the top. Then insert the bare wire end through the loop and release the clip. Repeat this with the other wire clip.

Next, connect the other bare ends of the wires to the appropriate terminals on your transformer. Wrap the wires around the binding posts clockwise, so they won't slip off when you tighten the thumb nuts. Your test track is now ready for use.

Track Profiles

First, however, you may be wondering about whether to use O or O27 gauge track. You may not know how they differ, or you may be uncertain about how to combine them. Let's take a few moments to shed some light on the situation.

Lionel has been manufacturing three-rail O gauge sectional tubular track in the same two profiles for more than sixty years. The track gauge (the distance between the running rails) for O and O27 gauge is the same at 1¼ inches. However, when assembled into a circle, O27 track has a

This photo shows the correct positioning of the lockon and connecting wires to a transformer.

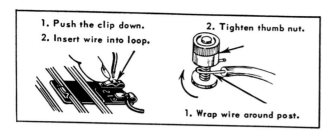

Attach one end of each connecting wire to the lockon and the other end to the transformer.

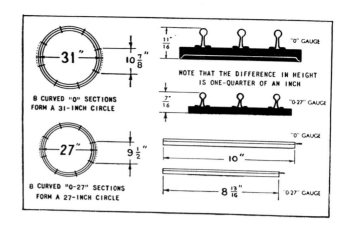

Comparison of the larger O gauge track with O27 profile.

27-inch diameter (hence, its name); O gauge has a 31-inch diameter. Furthermore, Lionel has always marketed O27 as its junior or economy line, which is why it designed the track sections to be smaller and shorter and made them from a lighter weight of sheet steel than was true with its O gauge sections. To be specific, O gauge track is 11/16 inches high, whereas O27 track is only 7/16 inches. A straight section of O27 track is 8¾ inches long, while an O gauge piece measures 10 inches.

Manufacturers continue to make O and O27 gauge track. Lionel LLC and MDK Electric Trains offer both lines in a variety of diameters to meet the needs of even the most serious layout builders. In addition to the original 27-inch diameter, O27 profile track is available in 42- and 54-inch diameters. O gauge track comes in diameters of 31, 42, 54, and 72 inches. Lionel and MDK also make track switches to match most of these.

Lionel never intended for its two types of track to be used interchangeably. That's why each line has its own track switches and crossovers. And though a number of attempts were made over the years to abolish one line in favor of the other or to combine them in some way, these efforts met with little success. Still, some hobbyists have managed to combine O and O27 track, especially on permanent layouts. Success requires a fair amount of bending, prodding, and shimming.

If you have to combine the two profiles, I recommend spreading the O27 rail to accept the larger pins found on O gauge track rather than trying to squeeze the O gauge rail to mate with the smaller O27 pins. Switches are another matter. I've learned that it's almost impossible to insert the pins from a piece of O profile track into an O27 switch without seriously distorting, disfiguring, or otherwise breaking the switch rails. I suggest using a short piece of O27 track as an "idler" section between them. I also recall somebody once producing "transitional" pins with different sized ends, but I haven't seen one of these for years.

Finally, O27 gauge track must be shimmed up to bring the rail tops in line with O profile sections. I suppose that's one reason quarter-inch plywood was invented!

Track Geometry

Sectional track layouts are based on the circle and the straight line. Circles are divided into eight, twelve, or sixteen equal segments, depending

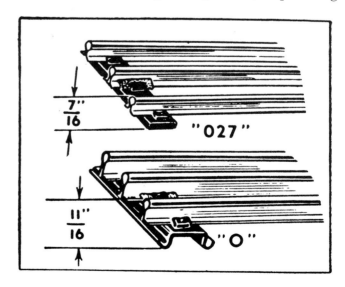

O gauge track is slightly higher than O27.

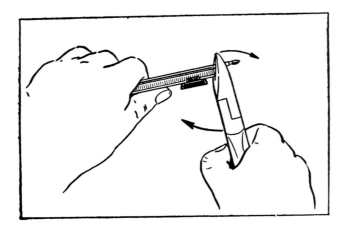

Use diagonal cutters when you need to remove a track pin.

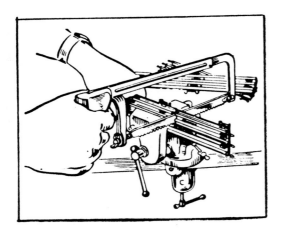

Use a hacksaw to tailor a section of track to fit.

upon the diameter. Straight lines, also of equal lengths, can be added to the circle, thereby changing it into an oval or something resembling a square, rectangle, or triangle. Simple layouts based on these geometric forms have been popular with beginners since Lionel started showing them in catalogs more than eighty years ago.

Tangents and intersecting lines are also common. If you put straight lines intersecting at right angles between two truncated circles, the familiar figure eight emerges. Then you can run tangents anywhere for sidings. You can create an almost infinite number of variations merely by rearranging the track sections.

However, the configurations of some layouts demand that you modify track sections in addition to rearranging them. S-curves and L-shaped designs require that you change the pins in some curve sections to make them fit. In such cases, you can best remove any interfering track pins with diagonal cutters. Instead of cutting the pin, grasp it firmly and lever the tool against the base of the rail. If you don't have diagonal cutters, use pliers to grasp the pin and pull it straight out.

From time to time, because of space considerations or quirks in the track geometry, you need to tailor a track section to fit the layout. You can cut sectional track with a hacksaw, one rail at a time or squarely across all three at once. Secure the piece of track in a vise, and clean up burrs with a file.

Adding track switches increases the operating potential of a layout, extending what J. Lionel Cowen called the "play value" of the trains. Industries on spurs can be serviced by the railroad. Cars can be stored in yards. Trains can pass each other on sidings or double back over return loops.

Track crossings ("crossovers") are made in 45- and 90-degree configurations. They make possible many interesting track layouts that can't be achieved with switches alone. Crossings do not require special wiring and can be inserted as any ordinary piece of track. However, unlike switches, the crossing length is not the same as that of a straight section, so track tailoring is often necessary.

Track Switches and Special Sections

Track Switches: Layout builders use track switches to change the route of the train. They install switches into the layout as they would any ordinary straight and curved sections, with each switch replacing one of each. Switches are manufactured in both manual and remote-controlled models in O and O27 profiles.

To control manual switches, operators rely on a lever installed on each switch to control the position of the swivel rails. Consequently, each switch must be within easy reach. By contrast, operators can position a remote-controlled switch, sometimes known as an "automatic switch," anywhere on the layout. It is connected to a control box via a three-conductor cable that can be of any length.

The most popular remote-controlled switches were, and still are, Lionel's 022 in O gauge and 1122 in O27. Lionel produced hundreds of thousands of each type over several decades with relatively little change. Because these two models are so common and widely used, I will concentrate my remarks on them.

Lionel designed the 022 to be deluxe in every way. Engineers installed heavy-duty solenoids in its motor mechanism to provide quick and positive action of the swivel rails. They added a lantern that rotates smartly with the movement of the swivel rails and indicates the position of the switch to the mythical little engineer in the locomotive cab. The lantern features a green lens for straight ahead and a red one for the curved route. Similarly colored lights on the control box relay the same information to the operator.

The 022 switch has a built-in non-derailing feature that uses insulated control rails on the divergent track routes to sense the presence of a train. It can automatically throw the switch to the correct alignment, if necessary, to avoid a possible wreck. For the switch to function correctly, the control rails must be separated from the rest of the track layout with plastic or fiber insulating pins, which are available at hobby shops. Ambitious operators may choose to power their 022 switches using fixed voltage coming directly from a transformer. This ensures enough voltage to make the switch snap smartly, regardless of a train's speed.

Hooking up any 022 switch is simple. Trace the three wires in the flat cable coming out of the control box, left to right, and connect them to the binding posts on the switch motor in the same order. The switch takes its power from the track unless you insert the fixed-voltage plug into the socket on the side of the unit. Doing so cuts off the connection between the switch motor and the track. The switch can't operate unless the plug is energized.

If the bulb is burned out, you can replace it by pulling the plastic lantern housing up and off. Controller bulbs are readily accessible. Replace all bulbs with those of the same voltage rating or manufacturer's model number. This information is usually shown on the base of the bulb.

The 1122 switch is a smaller, less-expensive version of the 022. It has the same features, performs the same functions, and hooks up in the same way. However, the 1122 does not have provisions for using fixed voltages and must rely exclusively on track power. Its control box is slightly different, too. Instead of having individual controllers for each switch, one controller handles

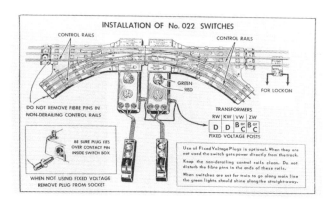

The lockon (far right) should be connected to the variable-voltage posts on the transformer.

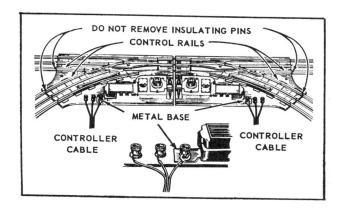

Installing Lionel's no. 1122 switches isn't difficult.

two of them. To replace a bulb, the operator removes the lantern casting and the screw holding the switch motor cover in place. The bulb becomes accessible once the cover is off.

Both the 022 and 1122 switches are usually durable and reliable. They tend to function no matter how old they are. If they've been stored for many years, however, they probably need to be worked vigorously for a while to get their parts moving again. To loosen everything, I suggest sending about 18 volts into them and working the controls a couple of dozen times. If that doesn't help, remove the motor cover, which on 022 switches is held in place by two screws on the bottom of the unit and on 1122 switches is held by one screw on top of the cover. Then shoot TV Tuner Cleaner (available at Radio Shack and other electronics stores) directly into the solenoid cylinders.

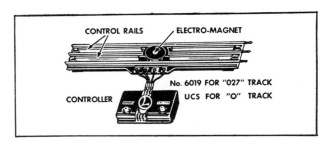

Lionel offered two types of Remote Control Track Sections.

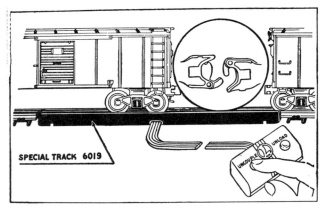

A push of a button is all it takes to uncouple cars over a Remote Control Track Section.

Next, work the solenoid plunger back and forth vigorously by hand until it moves freely.

This is a good time to lubricate the other moving parts, though not the solenoid. Put a drop of oil on the pivots and a dab of grease on the gears and latches. If you're working on the motor of an 022 switch, spray the moving contacts with TV Tuner Cleaner even if they aren't causing trouble.

Control rails on the 022 or the 1122 must have plastic or fiber insulating pins; otherwise, the non-derailing feature will not work. If these pins are missing, you'll hear the switch buzz loudly or chatter back and forth every time you apply power.

If problems persist with your switches after you've cleaned and lubricated them, consult a qualified service technician.

Remote Control Track Sections: These odd-looking pieces with five rails and a big, round (usually red) electromagnet in the middle come in O or O27 profile. When added to a layout, they replace one standard piece of straight track and are used to uncouple the cars from a train and to activate the electrical mechanisms in certain operating cars.

These sections, the most common of which are the UCS in O profile and the 6019 in O27, are connected via a four-conductor cable to a little black box with buttons marked "uncouple" and "unload." A press of either button, while the track power is on and the appropriate piece of rolling stock is in position, initiates the desired action.

Hooking up Remote Control Track Sections is simple and logical. Trace the four-conductor cable out from the control box, and connect each of the wires in order, left to right, to the terminals on the section. Many O27 units came permanently connected on both ends.

The most common problems with Remote Control Track Sections are those caused by a deteriorated cable or a control box that was taken apart by someone whose curiosity outstripped his skill at reassembly. The box contains layered wafer switches that must be aligned correctly and in the proper sequence or the track won't work. Replacing a defective cable can be tricky and should not be attempted unless you are patient and can solder wires in cramped quarters.

If you have serious problems with the control box or cable, take the unit to a qualified service technician and find out how much the repair will cost. Remote Control Track Sections are so common you may decide buying a used yet still serviceable replacement makes more sense.

Insulated Track Sections: Operators often use these track sections in place of Lionel's cumbersome 145C and 153C pressure-sensitive contactors on permanent layouts. These special sections, which have one insulated outside rail, can operate semaphores, block signals, gatemen, and a host of other trackside accessories.

Adding one or more insulated track sections to any layout, regardless of its size, is easy. The simplest method is to buy one of the ready-to-use insulated straight sections produced by Lionel and MDK. It's almost as easy and far less expensive to make your own sections. You can use any piece of track, straight or curved.

Start by taking a piece of track and removing one outside running rail. Use a screwdriver or knife blade to bend the tie clips far enough for the rail to come loose. Next, insert pieces of thin cardboard, electrical tape, or the third-rail insulation

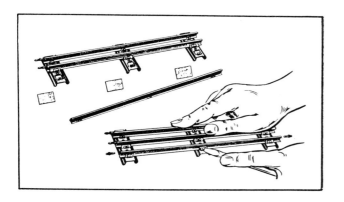

For an insulated track section, first remove an outer rail.

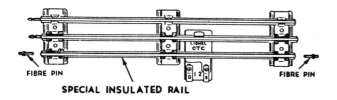

When finished, it has a fiber pin at each end and a lockon.

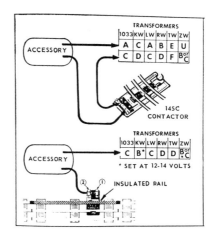

This diagram shows how an insulated track section can be substituted for a 145C contactor.

from a scrap section of track between this outside rail and the open tie clips. Then replace the rail and bend the clips back to their original positions. Do this gently so you don't damage the new insulation.

Be sure to insert plastic or fiber track pins into both ends of this rail to insulate it from the rest of the layout. Finish by placing a lockon between the center rail and the insulated running rail and connecting it directly to the accessory. The electrical circuit that powers the accessory is completed through the metal wheels and axles of the passing train, so the weight of that train doesn't matter.

Unlike contactors, insulated sections never get out of adjustment, though they must be kept clean.

Conclusion

Track switches, crossovers, and insulated track sections let you add variety and interest to a layout put together with sectional track. Still, I admit that regardless of how complex such a layout may appear, it always has a familiar, symmetrical, and predictable geometric pattern that you can't hide.

I couldn't care less about this, but it bothers modelers hung up on imitating all the bumps and irregularities found in nature. I think there's a basic honesty in using sectional track for toy train layouts that works as a positive factor. It's one of the reassuring pleasures and charming facets of playing with toys instead of exact scale models of the all-too-familiar and often dreary world.

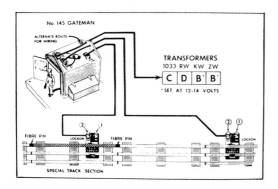
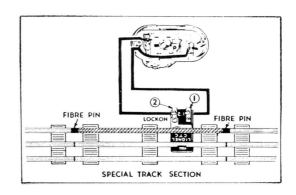

Operators use insulated track sections to power such popular accessories as the 145 automatic gateman (left) and 252 automatic crossing gate (right).

19

Chapter Four

SERVICING THE LOCOMOTIVE

Toy locomotives, which historically have mirrored the prototypes found on real railroads, were made in three basic types: steam, diesel, and electric. O and O27 versions of the latest, most powerful steam and electric engines were staples of the Lionel line throughout the prewar period. During the postwar era, models of diesels made by different companies joined the line. Even today, at the close of the twentieth century, toy train makers continue to produce detailed and smooth-running models of an assortment of steam, diesel, and electric locomotives.

Timelessness is one of the wonderful properties in the world of toy trains. There are no clocks, and there are no calendars. Smoke-belching New York Central Hudsons can run on the same layout with the latest General Electric Dash-9s without seeming to be out of place. Whatever type of locomotive you have, the most important point is to get it running. That's what it was intended to do. So, what are you waiting for?

Primary Maintenance

The first step in servicing your locomotive, whether it's steam, diesel, or electric, is to make a careful visual inspection of all its working parts.

Begin with the wheels; when turned by hand, they should rotate freely without binding. There should be no evidence of loose wheels or bent axles. Note that some locomotives were geared in such a way that the wheels can't be turned by hand. If yours is one of those, ignore this step.

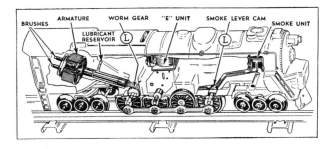

This cutaway view of one of Lionel's popular steam turbine locomotives (nos. 671, 681, 682, and 2020) shows its assortment of working parts. Points indicated with an "L" need to be lubricated occasionally.

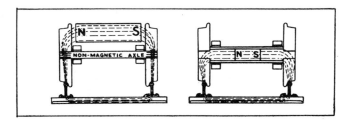

Magne-Traction is a patented method used by Lionel to increase the pulling power of its locomotives. A permanent magnet, installed in the locomotive's motor or axles, works in concert with the sintered iron wheels and ferrous metal track to form a magnetic field that prevents the wheels from slipping under load.

Use a Scotch-Brite scouring pad to remove dirt and oxidation from third-rail pickups and locomotive treads. Never use steel wool on your electric trains.

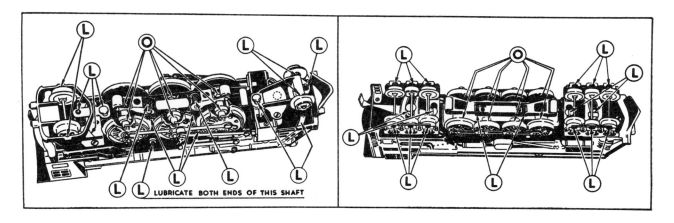

These diagrams show the main lubrication points on two popular styles of steam locomotives manufactured by Lionel. An "L" indicates points that need grease; an "O" indicates points that need to be oiled.

Next, check for loose, bent, broken, or missing parts, loose wires, and so forth. If your locomotive is equipped with Magne-Traction, look for stray metallic objects that might be clinging to the wheels, axles, or side frames and could get in the way or even damage the mechanism.

Speaking of the mechanism, this is a good time to clean it. I suggest you start by removing any visible dirt, grime, and caked-on grease from all accessible surfaces with a degreasing solvent, such as mineral spirits or rubbing alcohol, and many, many cotton swabs. Use these solvents carefully in a well-ventilated area because they're volatile and flammable. Be sure they have evaporated completely before you try to operate your locomotive.

Next, remove dirt and oxidation from the wheel treads and the third-rail contact shoes or rollers to ensure good electrical contact with the rails. A Scotch-Brite scouring pad works well for this task; avoid using steel wool. Follow up with solvent and cotton swabs.

The third step is to lubricate all moving parts. Put one drop of oil on the axles, shafts, and bearings, and a thin coating of grease on the gears. Be careful you don't apply too much of the lubricants because, when warm, they tend to thin out and run into places where they aren't needed. Consult the accompanying lubrication diagrams before starting.

A number of excellent lubricants are on the market, both oils and greases that are compounded specifically for toy trains. Use them if

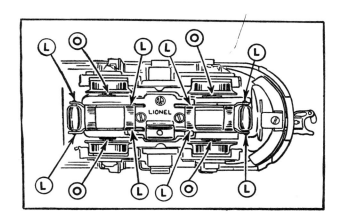

This diagram shows the main lubrication points on a Lionel diesel locomotive. An "L" indicates points that need grease; an "O" indicates points that should be oiled.

Lubricate your locomotive by putting one drop of oil on each axle, shaft, and bearing, and applying a light coat of grease on the gears. Oiling the armature shaft, shown here, is particularly important because that part spins so fast. Use oil first and then apply grease.

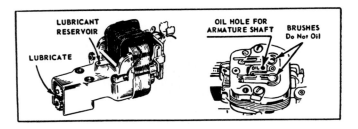

These diagrams show the lubrication points on some of Lionel's larger motors, which were installed in diesel and worm-driven steam locomotives.

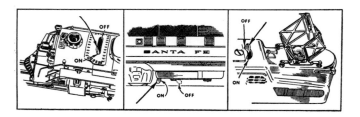

The cutoff lever for the sequence reverse mechanism is located in different places on Lionel's locomotives.

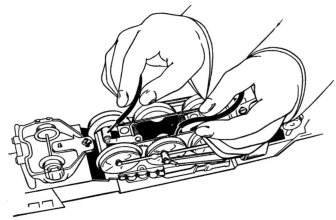

To troubleshoot a locomotive, touch the lead wires from the transformer to specific parts of the motor frame.

you have them, but almost any kind of general-purpose lubricant works. Household oils, such as 3-in-1 brand; white grease, such as Lubriplate; or even petroleum jelly can be used. Just use something! Apply it sparingly each time, but do it often. The major cause of problems with toy railroad equipment is inadequate lubrication.

Now you're ready to test-run the locomotive by itself. Put it on the track and turn on the power. Run it fast and slow around your test oval. Give it a chance to really warm up so the lubricants can penetrate the bearing surfaces. Let it run for at least ten to fifteen minutes.

While the locomotive is operating, make sure you activate the sequence reverse mechanism many times. After a long period of inactivity, it often needs to run through a number of cycles before it works as well as intended. Two basic types of sequence reverse mechanisms are in general use: the two-position kind and, more commonly, the three-position. With the first type, the locomotive goes from forward to reverse and back to forward again when the track power is interrupted. The second type features a neutral mode between forward and reverse. The sequence is: forward, neutral, reverse, neutral, forward, and so on. Most reversing mechanisms (known as "E-units" on Lionel products) have a lever protruding from the locomotive that can be used to turn off the sequencing feature. The engine then functions in only a single mode.

I can't emphasize enough the importance of putting your locomotive through its paces. Its performance should improve the more it runs. If that isn't true, please continue reading!

Trouble-Shooting and Making Field Repairs

What can you do if nothing happens when you put the locomotive on the track and turn up the throttle? Old Ray has some answers. First, check to see that the transformer plug is all the way into the wall outlet and the two wires leading to the track are fixed tightly in place. Now give the locomotive a helping hand. Tap it a few times. Push it around the track and it may wake up and start moving.

If the locomotive doesn't regain consciousness but its headlight is on, the sequence reverse lever may be in the off position, which means that your engine is stuck in neutral. Try pushing the lever back and forth a few times. Then, after disconnecting the two wires from the track lockon, turn the locomotive upside down. Touch one of the wires to any unpainted part of the motor frame. With the other wire, touch the center-rail power pickup roller or contact.

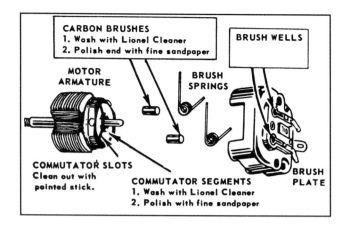

This exploded-view drawing shows the parts of a Lionel motor that should be cleaned. The brush wells should be cleaned with mineral spirits or TV Tuner Cleaner.

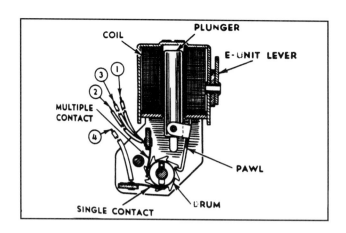

This cross-sectional view of a Lionel sequence reverse mechanism (also known as an E-unit) illustrates the areas that need cleaning.

Still no luck? Don't give up until you've tried a few more of my tricks. Hold the locomotive in an upright position and touch the wires again. Try different adjustments of the reverse unit lever. Should the locomotive run freely while being held in the air, but not when it's on the track, the trouble may be with the center rail power pickups. Because of wear or poor spring tension, they may not be making good contact with the rail.

Sometimes the motor will start and stop intermittently. If that's happening, look for a loose connection. Perhaps the wheels are turning, but oh so slowly, even at full throttle. That often indicates that the motor needs cleaning to restore its original power. Cleaning the motor isn't as difficult as it used to be, thanks to the invention of what I call "the tune-up in a can": TV Tuner Cleaner (available at Radio Shack and other electronics supply stores).

You may have to partially disassemble your locomotive to clean it adequately. If you do, take notes as you proceed so you can correctly put the engine back together. The points to be cleaned are the three copper segments on the commutator face, the three slots between them, the two carbon brushes, and the cylindrical wells in which they ride. After a locomotive has been used for a long time, a black gunk, composed mainly of carbon dust and stray lubricant, forms on these points. This ugly stuff reduces the efficiency of the motor by making the brushes stick in their wells and hindering the flow of electricity between the brushes and the commutator face.

Squirting a little TV Tuner Cleaner directly into the brush wells and onto the commutator face typically loosens the dirt. Then you can clean out the commutator slots with a wood toothpick or other pointed soft stick. If possible, spin the commutator as you spray everything again. Mop up the mess with cotton swabs. Repeat the spraying and mopping operation until the cotton swabs no longer turn black. This takes time and a lot of swabs, but it's much easier than the old way.

Of course, this cleaning technique may not significantly improve the motor's performance. Failure may indicate that the brushes or the brush springs need to be replaced, the commutator face is severely worn, or the armature has a bad winding. For any of these problems, I recommend that you consult a qualified service technician.

If the sequence reversing function works intermittently or tends to stick in one direction, the E-unit also might benefit from a few squirts of TV Tuner Cleaner. I suggest spraying the plunger, geared drum, and both sets of contacts directly. Then you should work the unit several times by hand and spray it again.

To get at the reverse unit, you'll probably have to remove the locomotive shell. This procedure is just a bit different for each individual make and

A pill-type smoke generator has been installed on this locomotive.

An SP smoke pellet is being put down the smokestack of a Lionel steam locomotive.

model, so detailed instructions aren't practical here. Generally speaking, diesels are easier to take apart than steam engines. Their shells typically are held in place with two screws or locking swivels at opposite ends of the unit. With steam locomotives, many of the mechanisms are held by screws through the top of the boiler casting, or underneath it, or both. Some have long transverse screws or pins that must be removed. They do come apart, and they usually can be put back together by retracing the disassembly steps. Once you have done it, you're an expert.

Study the locomotive first to see how everything fits. Look for the screws or pins that may be holding it together. Remove them one at a time and see what happens. You can't hurt anything seriously. These were mass-produced toys that required logical construction for efficiency on the assembly line. Use your own logic on them and you'll figure them out.

Often cleaning the reverse unit is all that's needed to get it clicking right. If the problem persists, see your service technician. Replacing this unit or key parts is a tricky operation that requires special skill and equipment.

Smoke Generators

Lionel steam locomotives used two types of smoke generators. Earlier models, manufactured from the mid-1940s through the late 1950s, were fueled by little white pills. Later ones, produced from the late 1950s onward, used a smoke fluid. Both generators were equipped with an internal heating element and relied on a piston synchronized with the motion of the drivers to produce a puffing effect.

Although neither type of smoke generator was trouble-free, the earlier ones are more often found inoperative today. Sometimes the nichrome heating element wires need to be replaced because they're burned out or broken. Most often, however, faulty smoke production is caused by a generator clogged with unexpended pill residue. (Kids loved dropping pills down the stack.)

In such cases, the cure is simple and painless: just keep running the locomotive until the pills melt. As this occurs, the volume of smoke will increase. It may take some time, so be patient and definitely avoid feeding the beast more pills!

Whistles and Horns

Whistles and horns on Lionel locomotives malfunction most often because of a broken pickup wire, dirty contacts on the activating relay, or a faulty controller on the transformer. If you're lucky, the problem is a broken wire. It's the easiest to resolve since it can be spotted by visual inspection and then replaced.

As for dirty contacts, you can remedy that situation by spraying them with TV Tuner Cleaner. Then you polish them with very fine sandpaper.

To determine whether you have a faulty controller, you need to test it by using another whistle or horn that you know works. Beyond this, an inoperative horn may be caused by a dead dry-cell battery, corroded battery contacts, or a defect in the horn unit. If the battery is the problem, just change it. If the contacts are the problem, just clean them with sandpaper.

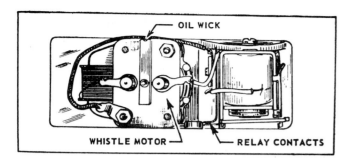

Looking at the air whistle unit of a Lionel steam locomotive, note the locations of the oil wick and relay mounts. These units always were installed in tenders.

The battery that powered the horn in Lionel's F3 diesels was located in the center of the frame.

Broken horn units are another story. They can't be repaired easily, though replacements are available from toy train parts dealers. Sluggish or noisy air whistle motors often can be helped by lubricating the armature shafts and bearings. I recommend the TV Tuner Cleaner treatment for this often neglected motor.

Bulb Replacement

A variety of bulbs can be found behind the headlight lenses on toy locomotives. Many of them screw into their sockets; others have a bayonet base, so they must be pushed down and rotated until they lock in place. Still others merely plug in. Be sure your replacement is of the same type and voltage rating. You usually can find this information on the base of the bulb. Otherwise, consult your dealer or parts supplier.

Once you know which bulb to use, replacement may involve partial disassembly of the locomotive. Diesel shells must be removed following the procedure outlined earlier in this chapter. With steam engines, you have to take off the boiler fronts or lead trucks. When the bulb is accessible, remove the old one and put in the new; what could be simpler?

That's it! As I've always said, old toy train locomotives are tough creatures indeed. While built to withstand rough treatment in the hands of children, they were also, in the process, built to

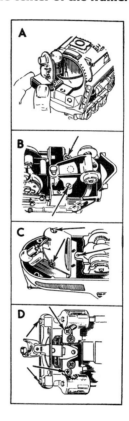

The headlight bulbs were located in different places on various Lionel locomotives. To replace some bulbs, you must first remove screws (indicated by arrows).

last. Many of them have survived the ravages of time in better condition than their owners. They require a minimum of care (often no more than periodic lubrication and occasional cleaning) to keep on going and going and going.

Chapter Five
PREPARING THE CARS

As you continue to dig into the box of electric trains you found or bought, you'll certainly come across some cars for your locomotive to pull. Once you've removed them, you can take a good look at them to see how their forms, colors, and other features differ. These differences mirror what you would observe on real railroads, where three basic types of cars are used. To learn more about your models, you need to be familiar with these cars, which can be categorized by their function or the cargo they're intended to carry. In American practice, these three types are rarely mixed in any given train.

The first and most plentiful type consists of freight cars. It includes boxcars, tank cars, gondolas, flatcars, hoppers, refrigerator cars, stock cars, automobile carriers, and the like. Until quite recently, a freight train always had a caboose at the end. Some still do.

The second type of railroad car is the passenger car, which is used to transport people and their belongings over short or long distances. Examples include Pullman cars, coaches, Vista-Domes, diners, baggage cars, and observation cars, along with various combinations of these. At one time, most railroads ran passenger trains; since 1971, however, nearly all the passenger equipment in the United States has been owned by Amtrak.

The third category covers work cars, which railroads use to maintain operations. Among the most common kinds of work cars are crane cars, searchlight cars, bunk cars, tool cars, and flatcars loaded with railroad equipment and supplies.

The world of toy trains has always respected these divisions. However, the imaginative designers working at Lionel and Gilbert added another creative dimension to them with cars that weren't passive trailers but reflected the world in a different way, made colorful statements, and captured the imaginations of the young. Few of these models had prototypes in the real world, yet that didn't seem to matter to the designers or the kids who played with what were called "operating cars."

These toys ingeniously added a wide range of action, excitement, and animation, not to mention an element of human conflict to the toy train environment. For example, flatcar loads reflected the gamut of sentiments that characterized the 1950s: fears of nuclear war and hopes for peace on earth. They carried everything from miniature missiles to Christmas trees. Some launched rockets and satellites. Others exploded on impact. The good guys chased the bad guys.

Interestingly, those cars of a more pastoral or domestic nature seemed to have a longer life span. The best-selling operating car featured a little figure who delivered cans of milk. Also popular was a stock car that featured rubber cows moving in

Throughout the postwar era, Lionel offered an amazing assortment of freight and passenger cars, work-related rolling stock, and operating cars.

26

and out of the car and a holding pen. Lionel marketed a number of searchlight cars, whose beams pierced the darkness so that crane car crews were able to get a wrecked train back on the rails at night. Still other mainstays of the postwar line dumped wood dowels or plastic coal into trays, or all over the living room carpet.

My favorite Lionel operating car was the 3434 poultry dispatch. It came with interior illumination so everyone could see that it was loaded with hundreds of chickens. At the touch of a button, the door on one side opened and a figure holding a broom stepped forward, as though he was sweeping the floor. This car said so much on so many different levels. I still chuckle at the metaphor.

General Tips

It isn't possible in an introductory book such as this to offer instructions or even hints on servicing or repairing all of Lionel's operating cars. Instead, I have selected a few of the more popular cars as representative examples.

Begin with a visual inspection of the car. You're looking for exterior damage and missing parts. If the car has interior illumination or an electrically activated mechanism, be sure that the wires to the third-rail or the pickups to the Remote Control Track are intact. If the car depends on a manually activated mechanism, test it by hand.

What if parts are missing? Fortunately, many of the fragile and easily lost parts from operating cars have been reproduced and can be obtained from hobby dealers and parts suppliers. Of course, the most important components of any car, whether it performs some operation or merely tags along behind the locomotive, are the trucks on which it rides. With toy trains, that usually includes the couplers.

Therefore, you need to examine the trucks carefully. They must not be bent or twisted in such a way that all four (or six) wheels are prevented from riding squarely on the rails. With a little patience and a pair of pliers, you can put distorted metal trucks back into shape. Plastic trucks are another story, but they usually break before they distort. If, however, you insist on trying to repair plastic trucks, I suggest heating them with a hair dryer and gently "persuading" them, though this technique doesn't always work.

Inspect the trucks on all pieces of rolling stock. Lubricate the wheels on a regular basis, but avoid adding too much oil. Use a toothpick to apply one drop of oil to each axle.

Experience has taught me that trucks should be mounted loosely enough so they can turn without effort or impediment. Give them the gravity test: turn the car from side to side. The trucks should respond immediately. Sometimes, adding a little grease between the trucks and the car body helps, but be aware that it can interfere with any electrical connections.

For maximum effect, all the wheels on a car should spin freely on straight axles. In the case of recent cars with wheels and axles permanently joined together, all wheel sets must spin freely within their trucks. Straight axles are indicated in either instance. With older metal trucks, you occasionally have to bend their sideframes outward to eliminate pinching and binding on the wheels.

Couplers are highly vulnerable to accidental damage because they protrude. Diecast knuckle couplers, riveted to sheet-metal arms, tend to break off easily. If that happens, you may be able to reattach them using epoxy cement or super glue gel. I advise you to use one or the other for this job because these two adhesives are not compatible.

Check next for couplers that are bent upward or downward and, therefore, can't uncouple properly or mate well with other cars. If you find one with this problem, you usually can bring it back into position by using needlenose pliers to adjust the sheet-metal arm rather than the coupler itself.

The knuckles on Lionel couplers are spring-loaded and designed to pop open when activated.

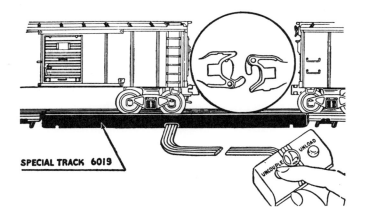

Maintaining couplers is important if you want freight cars to uncouple over a Remote Control Track Section.

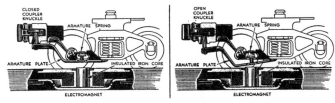

This cutaway view shows how a Lionel knuckle coupler operates on a Remote Control Track Section.

This action, admittedly a pleasure to watch, isn't operationally essential. The little springs usually break after a while, and the knuckles no longer pop open. When the coupler armature is pulled down by the electromagnet in the remote control track, the knuckle latch will release and the drag from the next car in the train will force it open.

Finally, remember that regular wheel lubrication is essential, particularly with older, heavier cars, for minimizing friction and easing the load on your locomotive. One drop of oil, applied at the axle, is all you'll need. Adding too much oil will cause it to run onto the tracks and create problems. Newer cars, equipped with fixed wheel sets, needle bearings, and Delrin plastic trucks, are designed to roll freely without lubrication.

Six Popular Operating Cars

Milk Car: Several versions, with different numbers and body styles, appeared over two decades. The man inside delivers milk cans, one at a time, to a loading platform. The unload button on a remote control track, positioned next to the platform, operates the internal car mechanism. Seven milk cans are loaded through a hatch in the roof while the car is on the track. Any derailment of the train or handling of the car while it's loaded tends to cause the cans to dislodge and jam up the action. Then the car must be taken apart to retrieve them.

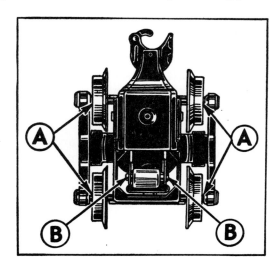

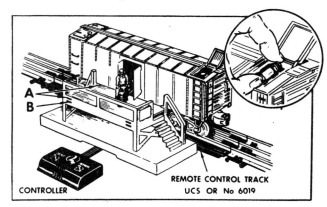

One of Lionel's popular milk cars.

This diagram indicates points of lubrication on metal trucks. Put a drop of oil on each axle at points marked "A." If the car has a center rail pickup (labeled "B"), be sure to lubricate that part as well.

Lionel offered two platform heights, depending on whether the milk car was used on O or O27 gauge track. Operators made the adjustment by slipping the platform into the correct set of slots: "A" for O gauge and "B" for O27 gauge.

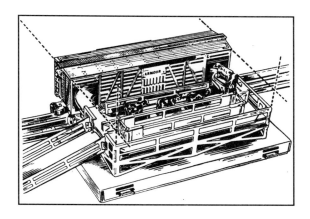

Operators of all ages enjoy Lionel's operating cattle car.

Cattle Car: A relative to the milk car in size and operating interest is the cattle car (no pun intended). It also has a trackside platform, but in the shape of a stock pen. Little rubber cows, lined up in the pen, are dispatched into the waiting car. Closing the door on the opposite side of the car keeps them in. The animals can be unloaded into the pen by opening the door. Or they can pass through the car and pen endlessly, if an operator desires.

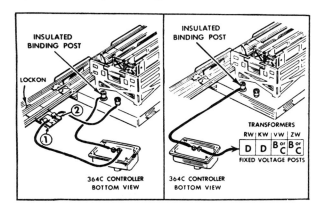

Hookups to the platform use track power or fixed voltage.

As with the milk car, the platform that comes with the cattle car has slots for height adjustments as well as different sizes of power blades to accommodate O or O27 gauge track. This car differs from its companion in not having to rely on a remote control track; instead, it has its own internal electrical circuits, so hookups use track power or fixed voltage.

The cattle car provides lots of fun and always pleases viewers. It works best if the track is perfectly level and the car is positioned exactly in place. Sometimes, as in real life, the cows develop stubborn streaks or minds of their own and have to be prodded into the car with a poke of the finger.

Searchlight Car: This basic flatcar with a plastic "generator" and a large floodlight, is perfectly at home in a work train. The big light rotates in all directions, which creates a dramatic effect in a darkened room. It can be turned on and off at the press of the uncouple button when the car is centered over a remote control track. The switch lever, located under the car, can be operated by hand, but that's not as much fun.

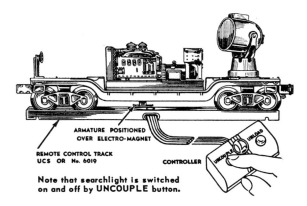

Searchlight cars were favorites during the postwar years.

Some versions of the searchlight car have internal motors to make the light housing spin by itself. I think they're intended for movie premieres and supermarket openings in Lionelville.

Barrel Car: Essentially, this is a long gondola with a load of wood barrels. At the touch of a button, the barrels begin to move along a metal trough on the floor, up and out of the car, and into a trackside bin. All the action takes place under the watchful eye of a little rubber figure.

A special OTC contactor came with the car, which also can be operated with the unload button of a remote control track. Make certain only one car truck is on the remote control section at a time. Otherwise, the mechanism will short out.

Lumber Car: Models that automatically unload logs (dowels) have been around for a long time. Some Lionel cars were equipped with electrical solenoid mechanisms that offered slower, more realistic action. They were operated by the unload button on a remote control track section.

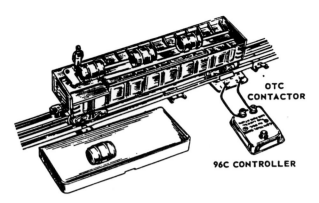

Barrel cars provided more freight activity.

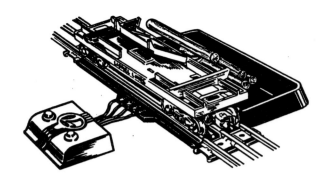

Dumping logs involved only the push of a button.

More recently, cars with spring-loaded dumping frames have taken over the market. They're operated by the uncouple button and tend to throw logs off the car.

Dump Car: The granddaddy of all operating cars first appeared in 1938. After World War II, Lionel designed more up-to-date models intended to dump plastic pellets of "coal."

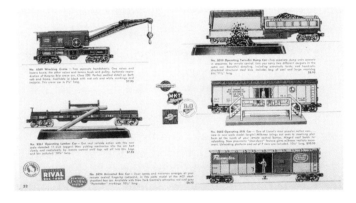

Many cars, including the operating boxcar, milk car, dump car, and lumber car, were updated in the 1950s.

Coal dumpers have always been big with kids because they could load them with so many other things: marbles, pennies, stones, and shells. The car's action is simple. Push the unload button, and a solenoid lifts the bin so that its cargo rolls or slides out.

Operating Boxcar: The simplest of all the action cars is the operating boxcar. It's a purely mechanical device that uses a single spring. The press of the uncouple button pulls down a plunger. This in turn opens the door, and a little man comes forward to look out the car.

There have been many variations on this one design. My favorite, the chicken sweeper car, used the same mechanism, as did a car in which the figure tossed out a mailbag.

So, now you have the transformer checked out and the track connected into a layout. You've cleaned and lubricated the locomotive and cars. Everything's ready to go, which means it's time to run your train. What are you waiting for?

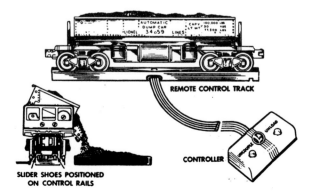

Dump cars worked great with Lionel's coal.

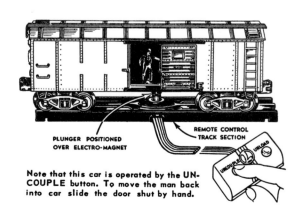

Operating boxcars added life to any Lionel layout.

Chapter Six

SETTING UP THE ACCESSORIES

To turn an electric train layout into something more than barren tracks on the floor, Lionel and some of the other toy train manufacturers produced a wide array of auxiliary items known as accessories. A number of accessories were merely passive trackside decorations that provided a setting of railroad atmosphere: tunnels, bridges, and station platforms come to mind. Others were illuminated, giving light and warmth to nocturnal operations.

As nice as it was to feature a tunnel or a set of streetlights on your layout, the most enjoyable and impressive were the accessories that actually did something. They augmented the sights and sounds, not to mention the action, that were part of "playing with trains." Operating signals and warning devices, cargo loaders, and animated stations significantly enhanced the illusion of reality on any model railroad.

This chapter contains instructions for wiring and operating ten popular Lionel action accessories. The first four are intended for use at grade crossings and warn motorists of an approaching train. The next two accessories are models of signals used by railroads to control traffic among the trains on the line. Next, there is machinery connected with trackside industries that's used to load and unload railroad cars. The last two accessories are miniature freight and passenger stations that serve as stops along the way.

To activate most of its operating accessories, Lionel provided pressure-sensitive contactors, which responded to the weight of the passing train

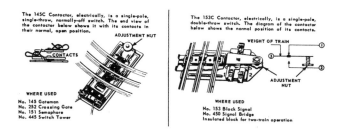

Lionel cataloged a pair of contactors for use with many of its operating accessories.

in order to start or stop the action. The two most common contactors are the 145C, which is a simple single-throw switch, and the 153C, which is a double-throw switch. As useful as these contactors are, their functions can be unreliable. Chapter 3 contains information on how to replace them with insulated track sections, which are more effective and reliable.

Four Popular Warning Accessories

154 automatic highway signal: A warning device found at grade crossings that still is widely used. As the wheels of a train roll over the contactor, the red warning lights of this accessory blink alternately, warning drivers that a train is approaching.

The signal is connected directly to the track by means of a special two-section insulated contactor (154C), which completes the electrical circuits to the bulbs.

140 automatic banjo signal: This type of signal, also known as a wig-wag, is common at grade

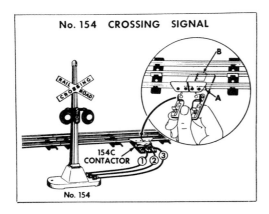

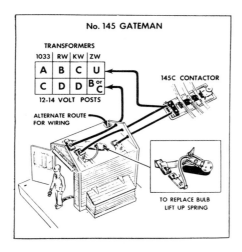

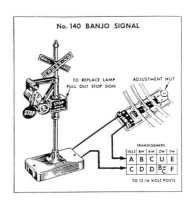

crossings, too. As a train approaches, the red warning bulb goes on and the arm begins to swing over it, giving the impression of a blinking light.

145 automatic gateman: Produced for more than sixty years, this is the all-time favorite Lionel trackside accessory. As a train approaches, the door of the illuminated shack opens and the gateman emerges, swinging his red lantern. When the train has passed, he goes back into the shack to wait for the next one.

252 crossing gate: As in real life, when a train approaches, the arm of the crossing gate lowers and two red warning lights turn on.

Two Popular Trackside Signals

151 semaphore: Seen less and less, this kind of signaling device once was used on railroads throughout the country. Usually, the semaphore arm is up and the light shows green.

As a train passes the signal, the arm lowers and the light shows red to warn other trains in the block. When the train has moved a safe distance down the track, the arm goes up and the light shows green again.

153 automatic block signal: Railroads, both real and toy, continue to rely on this signal. The green light usually is on. As a train passes the signal, the light turns red to warn other trains in the block. When the train has traveled a safe distance away, the light returns to green.

The 153 can be used to facilitate two-train operation. By installing an insulated track block

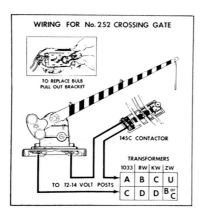

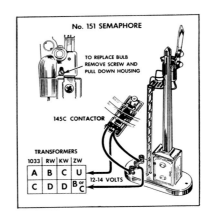

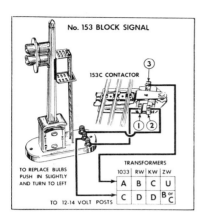

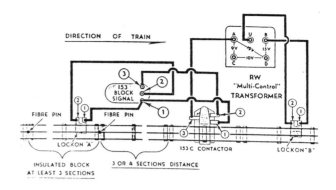

and using a 153C contactor in conjunction with it, you can run two trains on the same layout. Creating the block is easy. Just insulate a portion of track at least three sections long from the rest of the layout by inserting plastic or fiber insulating pins in the center rail at the ends of this block. Then connect the wiring as illustrated.

This diagram shows connections made to a Model RW or similar Lionel transformer, which has two different binding post terminals ("A" and "B") with slightly different output voltages controlled by the throttle. If you have a different type of transformer, an alternative wiring path is from terminal "1" on lockon "B" to terminal "3" on the 153C. The wire from binding post "B" on the transformer is eliminated.

Don't forget to lock the reverse units of both locomotives into the "forward only" mode. In addition, always try to have both trains loaded to run at about the same speed to ensure that the system works at its best. Then, as the first train crosses the contactor, it changes the position of the track signal to indicate "stop" and at the same time cuts the power to the insulated block. If the second train runs into the insulated block at this time, it stops and waits until the last car of the

Two-train operation relied on an insulated track block, a 153C contactor, and a 153 automatic block signal.

first train has cleared the contactor. Then it automatically starts up again.

Two Exciting Freight-Handling Accessories

364 conveyor lumber loader: The operation of this accessory, which is used with operating lumber cars, requires a Remote Control Track Section and a stretch of straight track. Log cars unload their cargo into a receiving bin placed at one end of the 364.

Then the logs are carried upward by a motorized conveyer belt to the other end of the accessory, where they automatically drop into a waiting empty car. A spotting light shows engineers where to stop when unloading each car.

397 operating diesel-type coal loader: This accessory moves artificial coal from a holding bin to a waiting empty car by way of a motorized conveyer belt. A Remote Control Track Section in front of the unit allows coal to be deposited into the bin from an operating dump car. The coal can then be reloaded into an empty car at a later time. The

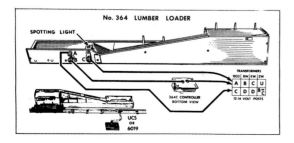

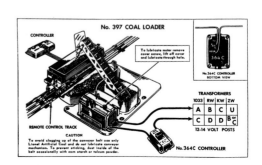

The 132 illuminated passenger station could be set to control the movement of a train.

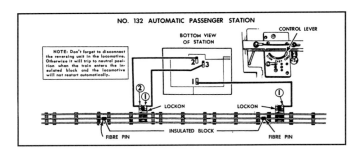

earliest version of the 397 came with a yard light; most did not.

Two Operating Stations

132 illuminated passenger station: This accessory is equipped with an automatic train control that stops and restarts the train in front of it. An insulated block accomplishes this action.

Operators control the amount of time a train remains at the station with a thermostatic switch that is regulated by a lever under the roof. When the lever is in the continuous-run position, the train passes by. The reverse unit on each locomotive must be locked in forward for this accessory to function.

356 operating freight station: This illuminated freight station is great fun to watch. Pushing the control switch causes the runway around the station platform to vibrate. That, in turn, causes two different colored baggage trucks to spring into action. The trucks move in and out of the station doors one at a time.

Parallel Accessory Wiring

Whenever several different accessories require the same fixed-voltage range, Lionel advises wiring them using parallel feeder wires from the fixed-voltage posts on the transformer (as shown below). This technique eliminates having a confusing jumble of wires hanging on the transformer.

I recommend that you use ordinary lamp cord or wires of a similarly heavy gauge for the feeders; solder them together if possible. You can add switches and their controllers to the same circuit. Remember that in parallel wiring such as this, the fixed-voltage value remains the same regardless of how many accessories you involve.

An alternative to this system that uses a common ground is discussed in Chapter 8. You'll find that common ground accessory circuits are convenient for permanent layout installations.

As you finish connecting your accessories, you'll see that we've accomplished a great deal in setting up and wiring a fairly basic toy train layout. Even better, your trains have been cleaned and serviced, so they're ready to run. All in all, we've made a tremendous start.

Where do we go from here? In the next two chapters, I'll explain in greater detail and depth how to plan, construct, and wire more complex and sophisticated model railroad layouts.

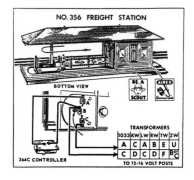

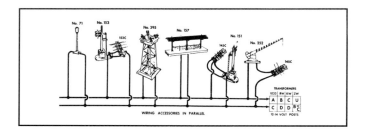

Use parallel feeder wires whenever you plan to operate a few accessories that require the same fixed-voltage range.

II. Track Layout and Wiring

Chapter Seven

Basic Layout DESIGN AND CONSTRUCTION

This section is intended for those of you who want more than a take-apart toy train layout that's open for business only during the holiday season or on long weekends when nobody else is at home.

Eventually, most people get tired of such transitory arrangements and yearn to have something more permanent: a designated space where the tracks are in place all year-round, providing a stage upon which the railroading drama can unfold at any time. Creatively designed scenery and set dressings supply a credible context for the activity: a real "slice of life" model railroad. This progression seems to be typical in the hobby.

Some enthusiasts refer to this phenomenon as being bitten by the railroad bug or virus, which is said to thrive for years in dusty old train boxes. I think that the instinct to build a personalized world in miniature goes deeper than that. It may even be genetic. Such creative urges can't be stifled without inflicting severe psychological injury. They can, however, be reasonably controlled.

I won't get into the politics of space acquisition and community property here, because every household is different. All the same, in most modern households, members consider space to be a valuable commodity that should be shared. No

This small layout, which was featured in *Greenberg's Model Railroading with Lionel Trains,* is filled with operating accessories, structures, scenery, and life! Viewers love watching all the action.

model railroad project was ever successfully completed without the full consent and approval of all the other residents at the address. Think about this before you contemplate knocking out a wall, annexing the guest room, or building a branch line over the laundry tubs.

I suppose these circumstances explain why trains were marketed for so many years as family

35

activities, and model railroads were promoted as projects that brought parents and children closer together by bridging the generation gap. This perspective has a way of freeing up room for a miniature right-of-way. You might at least try it before starting construction.

When title to the space for your layout is assigned free and clear, the first thing you should do is measure it down to the last inch. This is your operational universe, and in spite of Professor Einstein's theory, it's not likely to expand significantly during your lifetime. The best you can hope to do is use the space allocated in the most efficient manner.

The dimensions of that space will determine the kind of model railroad you can reasonably expect to build. You can't have a double-track main line with long, sweeping curves and wide, open spaces on a 4 x 8-foot sheet of plywood. However, you may be able to construct a credible yard and industrial layout or an attractive urban scene on which to operate toy trains in an enjoyable and challenging fashion. Be realistic going in and you will save yourself much frustration later on. This requires careful planning.

Initial Steps

Start with a pencil and a sheet of paper. Make a drawing, preferably to scale, of your space. One inch equals one foot is a good ratio to use for smaller layouts. Track planning templates in this scale are available from many hobby shops and train dealers. Modelers use templates much as craftsmen once relied on stencils: They insert a pencil into the opening and trace around it. Templates make it easy to draw track sections in all the available curvatures, along with lengths of straight track, switches, and crossings.

Those of you so fortunate as to have a lot of layout space at your disposal probably will have to use a smaller scale, perhaps a half-inch to the foot. If so, I recommend tossing aside your templates and resorting to a compass, protractor, and architect's scale. (Remember these handy tools from grade school? Now you know why your teachers taught you to use them.)

Your scale drawing should give an idea of how much is and is not possible to achieve within the available space. You may be in for a rude awakening or a pleasant surprise. In either case, you'll be armed with knowledge that can prevent you from making costly mistakes. I've learned that it's much easier to correct errors on paper than after they take shape in the real world.

Of course, if the actual floor space in question is clear of obstructions and you have enough track and switches on hand to set up a temporary layout, you may not need to work through the pencil-and-paper planning stage. Instead, you will be able to envision your track plan in three dimensions right from the start. Even so, you'll still probably want a rough plan on paper to show to friends and colleagues, particularly if you're seeking their help or advice.

Finally, bear in mind that you don't have to use *all* of your available space at once, although that temptation may be overwhelming. (Many people don't have this option, I know.) Some of the best layouts I've seen started out small and had future expansion in mind. As the time and money became available, they grew. However, the overall master plan was there in the first place.

Types of Layouts

Although the variations are almost infinite and often subtle, there are essentially only three types of layout designs: 1) Continuous Run, 2) Point-to-Point, and 3) Combination. All can have provisions for a train to change direction, pass another train, and spot cars on sidings, but that doesn't change the basic categories.

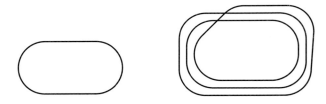

Continuous Run: By far the most common type of toy train layout, it runs the gamut from "idiot loops," where a locomotive appears to be chasing its own caboose around and around, all the way up to multiple-lap, over-and-under affairs that cross over themselves a number of times. The fundamental question is, will a train be able to run over the layout continuously without the attention of the operator?

Point-to-Point: This type of layout, also known as terminal-to-terminal, most closely imitates prototype railroad practice. Real trains typically run from one place to another. This fact makes such layouts popular with scale modelers and model railroad clubs. Operation is an intensive, hands-on occupation that usually requires timing and coordination among several operators on a fairly large layout. If you are inclined to build a point-to-point model railroad, it can bring a lot of enjoyment.

Combination: This kind of layout, which combines elements of the continuous run and point-to-point designs, is extremely popular. Three common variations exist.

First is the **out-and-back**, in which a train leaves the terminal, traverses the layout, and returns to the same place, but on a different track. To add realism, operators sometimes change the name on the terminal building while the train is on the road.

Second is the **point-and-loop**, which is like the out-and-back except that a train turns around on a loop and comes back on the same track.

Third is the **loop-to-loop**. This variation of the point-and-loop features loops at both ends of the line. This closely resembles a continuous run design, doesn't it?

Central Themes for Layouts

Chances are that in the area you have available, you won't be able to build the world in microcosm or even model an entire railroad line, regardless of how short it is. Your space doesn't represent very much real world acreage, even if you have an entire basement. So, you have no choice but to compress reality and be selective.

I recommend focusing on a single theme, locale, or type of railroad activity that you enjoy and designing your layout around it. Again there are three general categories: 1) Open Road, 2) Station Operations, and 3) Yards and/or Industrial Service. Builders of small layouts will do well if they concentrate on just one of these. Those of you free to plan larger ones may have the luxury of combining elements from all three.

Open Road: This theme is feasible only on large layouts, where trains can open up and stretch out while running through the countryside over wide-radius curves on nicely maintained roadbed. Speed, fun, and excitement result, particularly as you run sleek passenger trains.

Station Operations: This works well with medium-sized layouts. Trains arrive and depart according to a schedule, picking up and dropping off cars at the station. Traffic has to be directed, and operating problems need to be solved as they arise. Successful operation demands quick wits if you run on a tight schedule.

Yards and/or Industrial Service: This is a favorite for those who want to cram a lot of action into a fairly small space. Model railroads that follow this theme tend to be switching layouts. There, operators spot empty cars on industrial sidings as they pick up loaded ones. They assemble trains in the yards, waiting for the road engine to couple on and take them away. Meanwhile, other trains arrive and their cars are shuffled onto yard tracks, where they await towing to their ultimate destinations. Running a layout like this is a lot like playing chess. Every move has to be carefully contemplated and considered in advance. Still, the game can keep you pleasantly occupied for hours.

Track Switches on a Layout

The purpose of a track switch, on both prototype and model railroads, is to change the position of the running rails in such a way that the train is guided onto a divergent route. A toy train layout without switches very quickly becomes predictable and dull. Switches add variety and complexity to its operation.

In addition to providing the means for trains to take alternate routes, switches are necessary for

"spur sidings," which allow a railroad to pick up or drop off cars at trackside industries and to store unused equipment. Spur sidings have a switch at only one end.

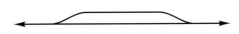

"Passing sidings" are similar, except that they have switches at both ends to enable trains to pass each other on single-track main lines. A faster train can overtake a slower one and pass it on one of these. Passing sidings are also essential when the main line is being used for traffic in both directions. One train waits "in the hole" (on a passing siding) until the train from the opposite direction has passed.

"Crossovers" are two switches positioned between parallel sets of tracks. Their function is to move trains from one track to the other. On prototype railroads, crossovers often are found in pairs.

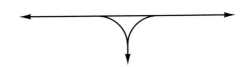

"Wyes" are track configurations that use three switches to enable mainline trains coming from either direction to take an alternate, usually perpendicular route. Trains from the perpendicular route can also move in either direction on the main line. Wyes, which take their name from their resemblance to the letter "Y," are often used in place of turntables to turn locomotives.

Generally speaking, "yards" are used to classify the traffic, put together outgoing trains or take apart incoming ones, park loaded cars awaiting pickup, and to store empty cars until needed.

"Single-ended" yards consist of a number of spur sidings that are accessible via a row, or "ladder," of switches at one end.

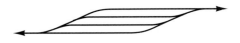

"Double-ended" yards are more versatile because they have switch ladders at both ends. They're usually found in locations that have a high volume of traffic in both directions.

A "terminal," as the name implies, is a complex yard facility at the end of a line. Terminals usually feature a number of spur sidings, passing sidings, and crossovers. In addition, most of them have some means of turning the locomotive.

"Reverse loops," which make it possible for a train to change direction without having to be taken apart, are rare on prototype railroads. They do, however, show up quite often on model layouts. Usually they're disguised behind scenery or hidden inside tunnels.

Track Crossings on a Layout

"Track crossings," which allow intersecting routes to meet at grade, increase the operating possibilities of a layout. They add excitement because of the element of potential danger involved.

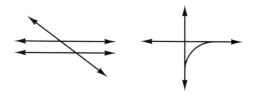

Crossings with 45 and 90 degree angles are available in both O and O27 gauge. They appear in some simple layout designs, such as the "figure eight," but are most fun when used in multiples or in conjunction with track switches.

Gradients on a Layout

Should your trains have hills to climb? Operators have debated this question almost as long as there have been layouts, with excellent arguments arising on both sides. I suppose it boils down to a matter of personal preference, along with the nature of the locale you're modeling. Mountain railroads usually have grades to negotiate, while those that are set on the Great Plains or in cities do not.

Having trains appear at different levels or elevations on a layout can be pleasing for viewers, but operational problems often arise with grades that can outweigh aesthetic considerations and even detract from the pleasures of operating trains.

I recognize that Lionel encouraged building layouts with stiff grades on them to show off the pulling power of locomotives equipped with Magne-Traction. The company even sold trestle sets to boost the elevation of one part of a layout enough to provide clearance over another part in the short space of eleven track sections. This was a great promotion for magnetically assisted traction when it was new.

However, many locomotive magnets have lost strength over the years. As a result, like the old gray mare, the locomotives "ain't what they used to be" in the hill-climbing department. Further, many locomotives still in service never had magnets in them. If you build a hill that's too steep for them, they will stall and sit there spinning their wheels in place and looking stupid.

Keep in mind that all trains, even those with good magnets, need constant throttle manipulation on grades. That is, they require an extra surge of power going up and a greatly reduced amount going down. Otherwise, there surely will be a disaster on the first curve at the bottom of the hill.

Minor derailments are also common at the crest of a hill and below, where the grade meets the flat table surface at the beginning of the climb. Some low-slung locomotives tend to short out at the same places. This problem relates to the way they were designed, so there isn't much you can do about it.

By now, you're wondering what my opinion is on the issue of grades. To be truthful, I've built layouts both ways (with and without grades) and confess that I have become an inveterate flat-lander. Give me the old "water-level route"; the other kind can cause too much aggravation.

However, if you still feel the need to elevate some portions of your track, please make the inclines as long and gradual as possible. Pay close attention to where the grades meet the flat surfaces. These areas have to be smooth, with no kinks or abrupt changes. This is best accomplished by using the "cookie cutter" method of construction, which I'll outline later in this chapter.

If you want one track to cross over and clear another, I suggest that you lower the bottom roadbed half way and raise the upper one by the same amount. This takes up a lot less horizontal space than if you merely elevate the upper track. You'll discover that such adjustments in roadbed height are easy to make if you use the "open grid" type of benchwork construction, also explained later in this chapter.

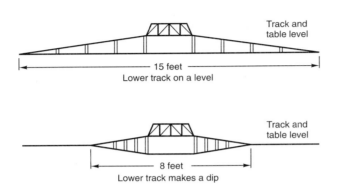

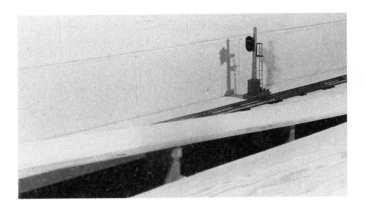

Here's a flat table-top layout under construction. The builder is using the cookie cutter method to elevate a section of the layout.

Building Benchwork

Model railroaders always refer to the base or framework upon which a layout is built as "benchwork." It doesn't matter whether you run your trains on a Ping-Pong table, an old garage door, or boards propped up by beer kegs—it's all benchwork, so get used to that term.

There are two types of benchwork most often used for toy train layouts: "table-top" and "open grid." Neither is difficult to construct, even if you aren't an experienced carpenter. Some layout builders elect to use a combination of table-top and open grid benchwork to excellent advantage. Others use what they call "cookie cutter" benchwork, which is a variation on the table-top type.

Whatever type of benchwork you choose, the key to success is making it sturdy enough to support trains, accessories, scenery, and your own weight. Eventually, you will probably have to climb on the layout to fix something.

Table-top: This is the easiest benchwork to build. Modelers typically use half-inch plywood, particle board, or wafer board; all of these work well as table tops, and they come in standard 4 x 8-foot sheets. They can be turned into respectable train tables of that size simply by framing the sheets with 1 x 4-inch lumber and putting in joists or cross braces every 2 feet for rigidity.

Homasote, a kind of glorified pressed cardboard, is also quite popular with table layout builders. When used correctly, it can deaden some of the noise that toy trains produce when operated. Because Homasote is lighter and softer than wood, it requires more joists: one every foot or so to get the same table-top rigidity. Some builders recommend putting a sheet of Homasote on top of the plywood or cutting out roadbed pieces from it.

Whether you use nails or wood screws on your table framework, I recommend that you also glue it. That will make the entire construction much more solid. Your train table can be supported on a pair of sawhorses. Or, you can build legs for it out of 2 x 4-inch wood. Finally, if you want a table of different dimensions than the standard 4 x 8 feet, most lumber dealers will saw the sheets to your specifications for a nominal fee. Then you can piece the sheets together any way you like.

Cookie cutter: This is not a separate construction technique, but a way of modifying flat tabletop layouts to provide for the addition of terrain features below the level of the surrounding ground. Builders use a saber saw to cut holes into the table top to make way for ravines, gullies, rivers, and lakes or to extend the contours of hills and mountains built on top of the table. They fit these holes with false bottoms and finish them when they install the scenery.

The cookie cutter method also works well for elevating the level of the track. Builders lay track on the flat surface first. Then they use saws to make cuts for several feet along both sides of the roadbed; this allows them to raise the entire section and ease the track into the grade.

Open grid: This is the preferred type of benchwork for permanent layouts. It is relatively inexpensive and quite versatile. Moreover, open grid benchwork lends itself well to almost any kind or shape of scenic terrain. However, it requires a bit more patience and skill at carpentry than does table-top benchwork.

On this open grid framework, joists have been placed across the L-girder frame

At the heart, this form of construction is an open grid of wooden L girders and regularly spaced joists and risers that is built over a framework that may be freestanding or attached to a wall. Builders install roadbed over the risers, which usually are a few inches higher than the level of the joists. There is no table; instead, you have an open lattice-work over which to apply the scenic terrain.

Over the years, several books have been published that explain the open grid method of construction and provide step-by-step instructions for building it. You'll find them listed at the back of this book. Don't undertake an open grid benchwork project until you've read at least one of these books.

Laying Track

On most layouts, even semi-permanent ones, the track is fastened to the benchwork in some

Risers to support the roadbed have been attached to joists on this open grid benchwork.

way. Modelers do this primarily to keep the sections from coming apart and to prevent the whole assemblage from sliding and wandering about on the table top.

Convenient holes in the crossties can be used to drive nails or screws through the track and into the benchwork. Modelers prefer screws, which can be removed easily without damaging the track if they change their mind. I recommend using ¾" x 4 roundhead screws for O gauge track and ½" x 3 roundhead screws for O27. One or two screws per section usually is sufficient.

As a general rule, you should make sure that the track grade is level and that the sections are snugly joined together. Lay long runs of straight

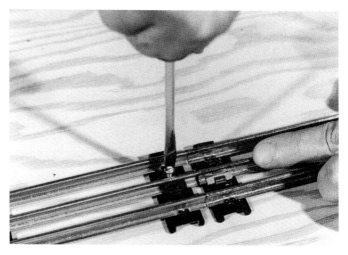

Track is screwed directly to the table-top benchwork.

sections with the aid of a yardstick or another straightedge to keep them in line. The job will look more professional that way. Also, if you're using insulating pins, check to see that all of them are in place before you fasten down the track.

You can screw the track directly to the benchwork or elevate it slightly by placing roadbed underneath. Prefabricated roadbed made of cork

Using prefabricated rubber roadbed adds a realistic look to the layout of your track.

or rubber is easily obtained from your hobby dealer. Otherwise, you can make your own using Homasote or roofing paper cut into the right configurations.

In addition, you can slip extra wood crossties of the same shape and color as the metal ones that hold the rails together under the track as you're laying it. This gives the end result a more realistic

You can easily shape commercial cork roadbed to follow the configuration of the track. Use small nails to hold the roadbed in place.

and finished look. Such ties are available commercially, or you can make your own by cutting strips of wood to the proper length and staining them to match. Six or eight of these per track section will do much to enhance the appearance of your layout.

Adding wood crossties under sectional track gives a nice finishing touch to any layout.

Creating Scenery

Scenery on a layout can range from simple to elaborate, depending upon your personal preference and level of skill or ambition. It can often be somewhat abstract, implied rather than stated. Building scenery is a way to express your creative imagination without having to acquire any new proficiency. The techniques for constructing the most popular kind of scenic terrain features are similar to those used in making papier-mâché, except that you work with different materials. Remember how much fun working with papier-mâché was in grade school?

Start by painting the table. That's a good idea anyway, as it will preserve the table and prevent it from warping. I suggest using flat latex paint in an earth tone, such as tan, brown, or green. You can go anywhere with a base in one of those colors; why, your layout will look good even where there's no scenery. Later, you'll add roads and other details by using a different color of paint.

Many layout builders use green indoor-outdoor carpeting with excellent results. They just glue it down and add details and structures on top of it. The nap of the carpet gives the impression of grass.

Other modelers create hills and mountains with the papier-mâché method. They crumple up old newspapers and fasten the wads to the benchwork with masking tape. Next, they prepare a solution consisting of equal parts of plaster of paris and water (two cups of each should be about right). Then they dip strips of paper toweling into the solution and lay them randomly over the newspaper wads. Some modelers substitute Hydrocal (made by U. S. Gypsum and available at most hobby shops) for the plaster of paris, as it produces a harder shell.

After the plaster of paris or Hydrocal has dried, builders apply earth-tone latex paint liberally over it. While the paint is still wet, they sprinkle a contrasting shade of Woodland Scenics ground foam (available at hobby stores) or dyed sawdust.

You can make tunnels in the same way, but instead of making the foundation from wads of newspaper and masking tape, use long strips of corrugated box cardboard that you bend into a half-moon configuration (so the inside is hollow) and tack to the benchwork. Then, after covering the track, you apply the plaster-soaked paper towels over the cardboard web.

You can be as intense or relaxed about this as you like. Experience has taught me that when imitating nature, you can't make a mistake. Somewhere in the real world, there's a precedent or prototype for whatever you might create.

Of course, you'll also need bushes, trees, and rocks on the layout. Take a tour of your favorite hobby shop for ideas and materials. There, you'll find the miniature people, animals, structures, automobiles, trucks, and other trackside incidentals that, once they're added, make scenes come to life. These details help give a layout its context and reason for being. For more information, consult the books on scenery design and construction that are listed in the last chapter of this book.

Sample Layouts

The track plans found on the following four pages first appeared in Linn Westcott's definitive book, *Track Plans for Sectional Track*, which was published by Kalmbach Publishing Co. back in 1956. Westcott, who was then the editor of *Model Railroader* magazine, put together 144 such layout designs, organized them logically from the simple to the complex, and published them in one complete volume that, unfortunately, has been out of print for many years. To make this rich resource useful to current toy train enthusiasts, I have selected an assortment of Westcott's plans for O and O27 gauge.

As you look over the track plans, you'll probably find many layouts that you would like to build as shown, as well as several that you would consider as models or frameworks upon which to create and try out your own ideas. Then you'll be able to conceive of and build a layout that meets your own specifications and requirements.

I find that many of Westcott's layout plans can be tailored to fit your available space simply by adding or subtracting straight sections here and there or substituting curves of a wider radius than the standard ones shown. Be aware that the letter "F" indicates "fitter sections," track that isn't of a standard length and so must be cut to fit within the layout plan. Commercially produced half-sections often can be used with minor adjustments to the overall geometry.

Finally, remember that you don't have to build your dream layout all at once. Some of these plans lend themselves to setting up the basic layout and then adding track, switches, and crossings as you go along. That's the beautiful part of using sectional track on a layout: It's so incredibly versatile and interchangeable. Just as you did as a youngster, you can easily alter your layout as often as you like.

Single-Track Layouts

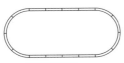

O27: 2'-9" x 5'-8"
O gauge: 3'-1" x 6'-5"
8 curves
8 straights

O27: 3'-5" x 4'-2"
O gauge: 3'-11" x 4'-9"
8 curves
6 straights

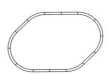

O27: 3'-3" x 4'-8"
O gauge: 3'-8" x 5'-4"
8 curves
6 straights

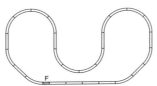

O27: 4'-0" x 6'-10"
O gauge: 4'-6" x 7'-10"
16 curves
11 straights
1 fitter

O27: 5'-8" x 5'-8"
O gauge: 6'-5" x 6'-5"
16 curves
10 straights

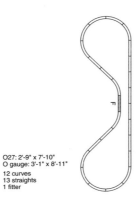

O27: 2'-9" x 7'-10"
O gauge: 3'-1" x 8'-11"
12 curves
13 straights
1 fitter

Double-Track Layouts

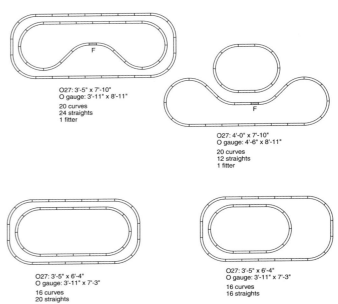

O27: 3'-5" x 7'-10"
O gauge: 3'-11" x 8'-11"
20 curves
24 straights
1 fitter

O27: 4'-0" x 7'-10"
O gauge: 4'-6" x 8'-11"
20 curves
12 straights
1 fitter

O27: 3'-5" x 6'-4"
O gauge: 3'-11" x 7'-3"
16 curves
20 straights

O27: 3'-5" x 6'-4"
O gauge: 3'-11" x 7'-3"
16 curves
16 straights

Layouts with One Crossing

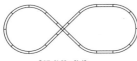

O27: 2'-9" x 6'-4"
O gauge: 3'-1" x 7'-3"
12 curves
6 straights
1 crossing

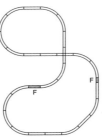

O27: 4'-9" x 5'-3"
O gauge: 5'-5" x 6'-1"
16 curves
6 straights
2 fitters
1 crossing

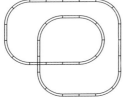

O27: 4'-11" x 5'-8"
O gauge: 5'-7" x 6'-5"
16 curves
14 straights
1 crossing

Layouts with Two Crossings

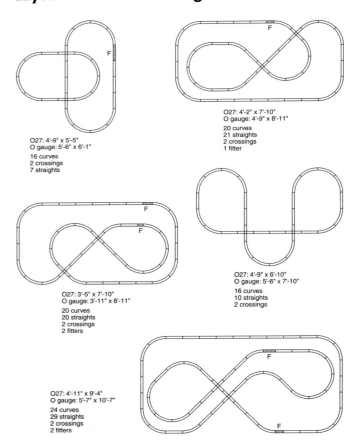

O27: 4'-9" x 5'-5"
O gauge: 5'-6" x 6'-1"
16 curves
2 crossings
7 straights

O27: 4'-2" x 7'-10"
O gauge: 4'-9" x 8'-11"
20 curves
21 straights
2 crossings
1 fitter

O27: 3'-5" x 7'-10"
O gauge: 3'-11" x 8'-11"
20 curves
20 straights
2 crossings
2 fitters

O27: 4'-9" x 6'-10"
O gauge: 5'-6" x 7'-10"
16 curves
10 straights
2 crossings

O27: 4'-11" x 9'-4"
O gauge: 5'-7" x 10'-7"
24 curves
29 straights
2 crossings
2 fitters

Layouts with One Pair of Switches

O27: 2'-9" x 4'-2"
O gauge: 3'-1" x 4'-9"
10 curves
4 straights
1 pr. switches

O27: 3'-5" x 4'-2"
O gauge: 3'-11" x 4'-9"
7 curves
6 straights
1 pr. switches

O27: 3'-5" x 4'-2"
O gauge: 3'-11" x 4'-9"
10 curves
7 straights
1 pr. switches

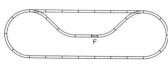

O27: 2'-9" x 7'-10"
O gauge: 3'-1" x 8'-11"
10 curves
15 straights
1 fitter
1 pr. switches

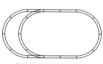

O27: 2'-9" x 4'-11"
O gauge: 3'-1" x 5'-7"
10 curves
4 straights
1 pr. switches

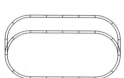

O27: 3'-5" x 5'-8"
O gauge: 3'-11" x 6'-5"
10 curves
12 straights
1 pr. switches

O27: 3'-3" x 6'-4"
O gauge: 3'-8" x 7'-3"
8 curves
13 straights
1 fitter
1 pr. switches

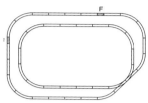

O27: 4'-6" x 6'-8"
O gauge: 5'-1" x 7'-7"
14 curves
22 straights
2 fitters
1 pr. switches

Layouts with One Pair of Switches and One Crossing

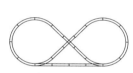

O27: 2'-9" x 5'-8"
O gauge: 3'-1" x 6'-5"
10 curves
6 straights
1 crossing
1 pr. switches

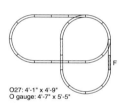

O27: 4'-1" x 4'-9"
O gauge: 4'-7" x 5'-5"
12 curves
4 straights
1 crossing
2 fitters
1 pr. switches

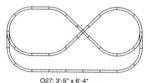

O27: 3'-5" x 6'-4"
O gauge: 3'-11" x 7'-3"
14 curves
11 straights
1 crossing
1 pr. switches

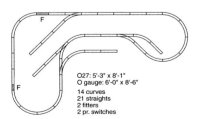

O27: 4'-1" x 7'-0"
O gauge: 4'-7" x 8'-0"
14 curves
10 straights
1 crossing
3 fitters
1 pr. switches

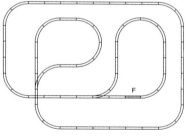

O27: 6'-4" x 8'-7"
O gauge: 7'-3" x 9'-9"
24 curves
35 straights
1 crossing
1 pr. switches
1 fitter

Layouts with Two Pairs of Switches

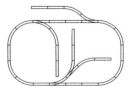

O27: 4'-1" x 5'-8"
O gauge: 4'-7" x 6'-5"
11 curves
14 straights
2 pr. switches

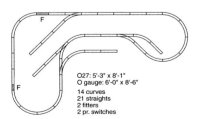

O27: 5'-3" x 8'-1"
O gauge: 6'-0" x 8'-6"
14 curves
21 straights
2 fitters
2 pr. switches

O27: 4'-10" x 5'-6"
O gauge: 5'-5" x 6'-1"
10 curves
13 straights
2 pr. switches

O27: 4'-2" x 4'-2"
O gauge: 4'-9" x 4'-9"
11 curves
10 straights
2 pr. switches

Layouts with Two Pairs of Switches

O27: 4'-11" x 4'-11"
O gauge: 5'-7" x 5'-7"
12 curves
14 straights
2 pr. switches

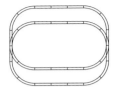

O27: 4'-2" x 5'-8"
O gauge: 4'-9" x 6'-5"
12 curves
16 straights
2 pr. switches

O27: 3'-9" x 6'-4"
O gauge: 4'-3" x 7'-3"
8 curves
16 straights
2 fitters
2 pr. switches

O27: 4'-11" x 6'-4"
O gauge: 5'-7" x 7'-3"
16 curves
22 straights
2 pr. switches

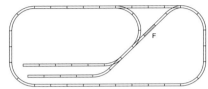

O27: 4'-2" x 9'-3"
O gauge: 4'-9" x 10'-8"
10 curves
32 straights
2 pr. switches
1 fitter

Layouts with Two Pairs of Switches and One Crossing

O27: 3'-5" x 6'-4"
O gauge: 3'-11" x 7'-3"
8 curves
10 straights
2 pr. switches
1 crossing

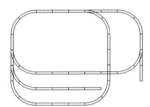

O27: 4'-11" x 6'-4"
O gauge: 5'-7" x 7'-3"
12 curves
21 straights
2 pr. switches
1 crossing

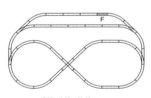

O27: 4'-0" x 6'-4"
O gauge: 4'-6" x 7'-3"
14 curves
14 straights
2 pr. switches
1 crossing
1 fitter

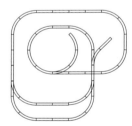

O27: 5'-8" x 5'-8"
O gauge: 6'-5" x 6'-5"
20 curves
15 straights
2 pr. switches
1 crossing

Layouts with Two Pairs of Switches and Two Crossings

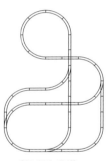

O27: 4'-11" x 6'-10"
O gauge: 5'-7" x 7'-9"
18 curves
13 straights
2 crossings
2 pr. switches

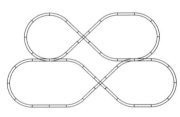

O27: 4'-9" x 7'-10"
O gauge: 5'-6" x 8'-11"
20 curves
12 straights
2 crossings
2 pr. switches

Layouts with Three Pairs of Switches

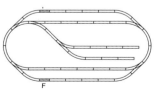

O27: 3'-9" x 7'-1"
O gauge: 4'-3" x 8'-1"
9 curves
27 straights
3 pr. switches
2 fitters

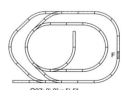

O27: 3'-9" x 5'-5"
O gauge: 4'-3" x 6'-2"
15 curves
12 straights
3 pr. switches
1 fitter

Layouts with Three Pairs of Switches and One Crossings

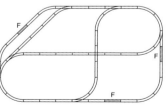

O27: 4'-9" x 7'-8"
O gauge: 5'-5" x 8'-9"
11 curves
21 straights
3 pr. switches
1 crossing
3 fitters

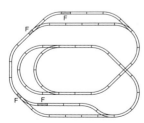

O27: 5'-0" x 6'-2"
O gauge: 5'-8" x 7'-0"
19 curves
19 straights
3 pr. switches
1 crossing
4 fitters

Layouts with Three Pairs of Switches and Crossings

Layouts with Four Pairs of Switches

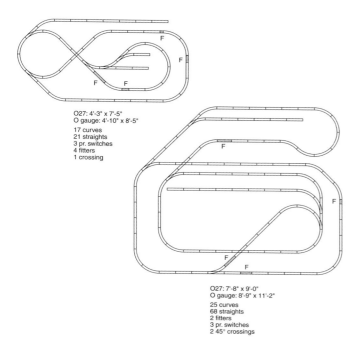

O27: 4'-3" x 7'-5"
O gauge: 4'-10" x 8'-5"
17 curves
21 straights
3 pr. switches
4 fitters
1 crossing

O27: 7'-8" x 9'-0"
O gauge: 8'-9" x 11'-2"
25 curves
68 straights
2 fitters
3 pr. switches
2 45° crossings

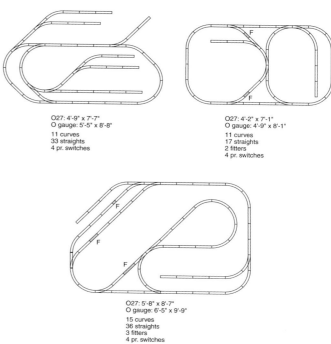

O27: 4'-9" x 7'-7"
O gauge: 5'-5" x 8'-8"
11 curves
33 straights
4 pr. switches

O27: 4'-2" x 7'-1"
O gauge: 4'-9" x 8'-1"
11 curves
17 straights
2 fitters
4 pr. switches

O27: 5'-8" x 8'-7"
O gauge: 6'-5" x 9'-9"
15 curves
36 straights
3 fitters
4 pr. switches

O27: 3'-9" x 16'-0"
O gauge: 4'-0" x 18'-3"
12 curves
24 straights
1 fitter
1 crossing
4 pr. switches

Layouts with Four Pairs of Switches and One Crossings

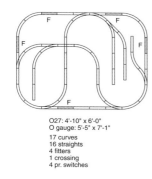

O27: 4'-10" x 6'-0"
O gauge: 5'-5" x 7'-1"
17 curves
16 straights
4 fitters
1 crossing
4 pr. switches

Layouts with Five Pairs of Switches

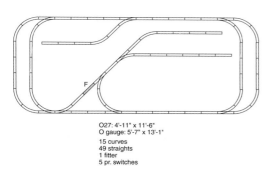

O27: 4'-11" x 11'-6"
O gauge: 5'-7" x 13'-1"
15 curves
49 straights
1 fitter
5 pr. switches

Layouts with Five Pairs of Switches and One Crossing

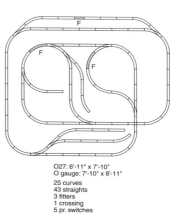

O27: 6'-11" x 7'-10"
O gauge: 7'-10" x 8'-11"
25 curves
43 straights
3 fitters
1 crossing
5 pr. switches

Chapter Eight
BASIC LAYOUT WIRING

The thrust of this chapter may seem strange in this age of digital electronics, with several systems of walkaround command and computer control available for model railroad layouts. These new technologies appear to work well, at least the ones that I've seen, but they are imponderably complex and can be a source of frustration for most ordinary mortals. For example, one manufacturer claims that its system is capable of controlling *ninety-nine* locomotives! So what? Who needs all that? There are more reserve options, modes, gimmicks, bells, whistles and blinking lights built-in than anyone could possibly need for running anything short of a space shuttle mission. And it wouldn't hurt to have Mr. Spock or Scotty from *Star Trek* with you to explain how it all works. The instructions, at least the portions written in English, aren't much help unless you're already at least a junior-level computer hacker.

Need I add that all these systems are usually expensive?

That's why I'm happy to report that the old conventional transformer technology, using block and cab control, is still around and serviceable at more reasonable prices. Both block and cab control can actually be more fun because they are hands-on systems, meaning operators have to be attentive at all times. And the basic concepts involved are easy to grasp, even for those of us who aren't rocket scientists:

1. If power is going to the track, the train will run.
2. The speed of the train is determined by the amount of power going to the track.
3. When the power to the track is shut off, the train will stop.

That's all there is to it. If you find yourself confused at any point in this chapter and want to give up and call an electrician, review the explanations of "transformer types" and "transformer hookups" in Chapter 2 and look ahead to the section on "elementary electricity" in Chapter 10. Meanwhile, I will try to explain each facet of layout wiring as clearly as I can while we move along.

Dividing Up the Layout

If you intend to run just one train around your layout and have no plans to expand your locomotive roster in the future, your needs are simple. You require nothing more than two wires connected to the track and perhaps a few feeder wires to boost the power at the far side of the layout.

However, if you ever plan to run more than one train with conventional transformer control, you have to divide the layout into blocks, or "zones of control," to prevent the trains from running into each other. A block is nothing more than an insulated stretch of track that's connected to either its own on-off toggle switch or its own separate transformer throttle. To independently slow the speed or stop the train within the block, turn the throttle down or throw the toggle switch to the "off" position. See how easily that works? Some of the larger transformers have more than one throttle built-in for this reason.

To make an insulated block, pull the steel track pins from the center rail of the track sections at both ends of the run you want to insulate and insert fiber or nylon pins instead. (These are available from your hobby dealer.) The two outside or running rails retain their metal pins. That's all there is to it.

How long should these blocks be? It depends on the size of the layout, the density of traffic, the average train length, and the location of yards, sidings, and stations. Blocks need not all be of the same length, but they should be at least as long as your shortest mainline siding.

How many blocks are necessary? Again there are only rules of thumb. Ideally, there should be at least three mainline blocks for two-train operation on it. More are probably better. I suggest having at least one unoccupied block at all times; it can serve as a buffer zone between moving trains.

Generally speaking, track switches are good locations to begin and end blocks because they usually indicate the boundaries between the main line and alternate routes, yards, and sidings. Also, you can easily spot the location of switches from the control panel, even in the heat of operation.

At least one track of each passing siding should be a separate block to allow one train to wait while another passes. In fact, you may decide to make both such tracks insulated blocks, particularly if the siding is a long one. Further, yards and industrial complexes that are large enough to permit switching operations without interfering with the main line should also be separate blocks. Finally, in some cases, you need to insulate individual spurs. For example, each track of a locomotive storage facility ought to have its own toggle switch to prevent waiting engines from moving until they're needed.

If you eventually plan to go with one of the new control systems, you'll discover that dividing your layout into blocks makes good sense anyway. With each block having its own feeder wire, the voltage drop caused by rail resistance in larger layouts will be minimized.

Blocking also makes troubleshooting easier. Suppose one block has a short circuit: You simply turn toggle switches on and off until you locate the block with the short. When you convert to the new technology, all you have to do is turn all the toggles to the "on" position or to the same cab and then hook the electronic components to the layout as directed. The old system remains as a backup.

Elementary Block and Cab Control Systems

"Block control" involves only one transformer control center, or "cab." The track layout is divided into insulated segments, or blocks, each having its own on-off (single-pole single-throw) toggle switch or speed-controlling rheostat. Operators keep trains from running into each other by manipulating the current in the appropriate blocks: turning it off or reducing it to avoid mishaps.

With "cab control" there are two or more transformer control centers, or cabs, which can be operated by two or more people. The layout is divided into the same type of insulated blocks, but each block is connected to all the cabs through separate single-pole single-throw toggle switches in each cab. The cabs are electrically identical and autonomous, each capable of running the entire layout. As a result, the engineer in the cab is able to take his individually assigned train over the whole

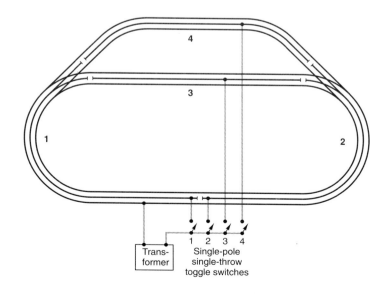

Block control using single-pole single-throw switches.

49

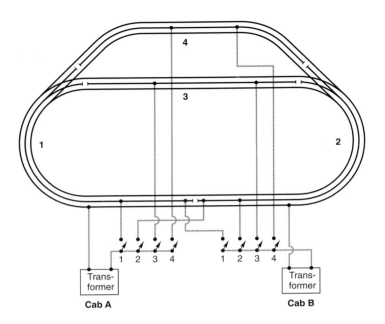

Cab control using single-pole single-throw toggle switches.

Cab control using rotary switches.

layout simply by energizing the appropriate blocks with his toggle switches.

According to usual cab control operating procedure, an engineer may energize only two blocks

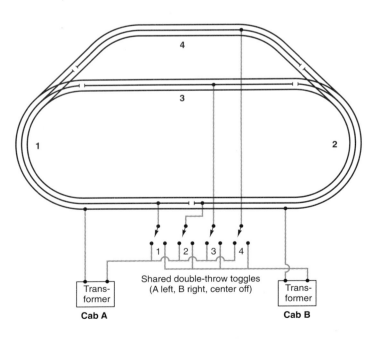

Cab control using single-pole double-throw toggle switches.

at a time: the block occupied by the train and the one ahead of it. The block the train has passed through must be shut off when the one ahead is turned on, because that same block conceivably could be fed by two cabs at once, which would have strange, even disastrous consequences!

Two popular variations on cab control switching deserve mention here. The first involves the use of rotary switches instead of toggles in each cab. This system requires sharp eyes and fast reflexes on the part of the engineer, who must rotate the switch knob to the next position at the exact moment the train is moving from one block to the next.

The second variation is feasible when there are only two cabs and both are in close proximity to each other. Instead of using single-pole single-throw on-off switches in both cabs, an operator installs one set of single-pole double-throw switches with "off" positions in the center for common use by both cabs. Then an engineer can select the block he wants to energize by throwing the appropriate switch in his direction.

The same procedures apply with regard to using only two blocks at a time and turning off the rest, even though both cabs couldn't possibly feed the same block simultaneously. There is often some confusion and fumbling at the shared portion of the control panel as both engineers try to manipulate the same row of toggle switches. It helps if one of them is right-handed and the other is left-handed.

Individual Transformers for Each Block

My favorite control system is the embodiment of simplicity and economy. It's a variation on conventional block control that uses a battery of small transformers, one for each block, instead of one large transformer and a series of toggle switches. With it, each block has its own individual speed control, whistle control, and reversing button, so one train can be slowed down realistically to prevent an accident with another, rather than going through the model railroad equivalent of an emergency air brake stop each time a toggle switch is thrown.

Onboard train whistles or horns can be activated individually, instead of having all of them blow at once, with the resulting slowdown of every train on the layout. Because each block has its own reversing control, the E-unit sequence reverse mechanisms need not be locked into the "forward only" mode, as they usually are with conventional block and cab control.

Each transformer powers one block of track, nothing more. You can use other small transformers for fixed-voltage accessory circuits and other electrical requirements. In addition, you usually need several different fixed-voltage values for the various lights and accessories. Set them up on their individual transformer circuits and forget them. (I use about 15 volts for accessories and 10 volts for lights: The bulbs last longer that way.)

Besides the versatility this system offers, the dollar savings can be substantial. Small transformers (those having fewer than 100 watts) aren't highly prized by operators or dealers, so often they can be picked up at very reasonable prices. As important, the supply of these transformers is immense: Lionel made them by the millions, and most of them still work. By way of price comparison in today's market, one new electronic command control system, with two remote cabs and 135 watts of base power, sells for $770; and one used Lionel ZW transformer, with four control throttles and 275 watts of power, is priced at $300

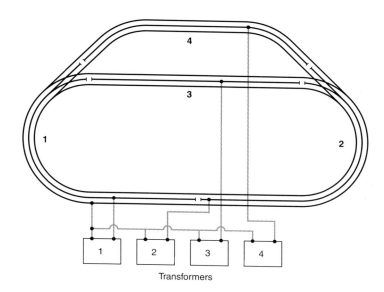

Individual transformer control for each block.

to $350. However, ten used 60- to 75-watt transformers with whistle controls can provide 600 to 750 watts in aggregate for $100 to $150. Enough said? That fact should send you out scouting the swap meets for treasures. (Test the transformers before you take them home!)

Lionel's small transformers don't all have to be of the same type or vintage to work, although having a lineup of similar units has a certain visual appeal. Their wattage ratings should be close to each other so there won't be a big difference in energy level as the train moves from block to block.

One of the best medium-sized layouts of the kind I've described in this book used eight of Lionel's small transformers from the early 1960s: six 1063s (each having 75 watts with whistle controls) on the track circuits and two 1073s (60 watts) for the accessories. All of these transformers had similarly shaped black plastic cases, so they looked very nice together.

The 1063 and the earlier metal-cased 1042 transformer work well in this application. Both are rated at 75 watts, feature whistle controls, and can handle 3 to 4 amps. Yet they look like so many other small transformers and usually are regarded as nothing more by dealers. At the going rate of about $15.00 each, they stand out among the dwindling list of bargains in the toy train world.

The 1033 and later 1044 may be the best units for multiple-transformer layouts, but they cost much more and the power advantage isn't commensurate with the price differential. They're rated at 90 watts each and boast whistle control and a load of 5 amps. Looking like big transformers, they are in great demand.

Accustomed as most people are to seeing large transformers connected to layouts, they're amazed at how well this system works. Since only one train operates within each block, 75 watts are more than adequate to run it, as long as it is kept lubricated and maintained. To minimize power loss, be sure to limit block length to about twenty tightly joined track sections and use heavy feeder wires (14 or 16 gauge). Switch motors, uncoupling tracks, and all operating and illuminated accessories are powered by their own transformer(s). Only the train draws current in each block. That's the secret of it. The best part is, as the layout grows, you have only more small transformers to buy to keep it powered.

Transformer Phasing

Whenever you use two or more transformers on the same layout, you must keep them "in phase" with each other. This means plugging all the two-pronged transformer cords into electrical outlets in the same way. Correct phasing ensures that trains pass smoothly from one insulated block to another. Incorrect phasing of the transformers causes locomotives to balk, arc, or stall at the transition points between blocks. It also can cause some accessories to operate badly or short out.

So how, you're probably asking, can you be sure all the transformers are in phase? Because phasing involves several transformer cords, I recommend using a multiple-outlet power strip

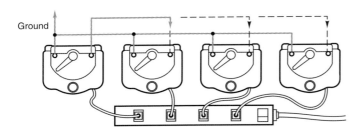

Transformer phasing is useful for multiple-train operation.

equipped with a master switch and a built-in circuit breaker. That way, all the plugs can remain inserted the right way once they're put into phase with each other, and the master switch can be used to turn the transformers on and off at the same time. The circuit breaker provides additional overload protection; you really can't be too careful.

To phase the transformers, start by connecting all the "ground" terminals together with heavy wire. Some transformers have a designated or recommended ground terminal, though most small ones do not. (Consult the chart under Using a Common Ground below to determine if your transformer is included.) Check your transformer carefully to see whether the binding posts are marked in this way. If they aren't, you can use any terminal as the ground as long as your wiring is consistent among all the transformers in the system. For the illustration, I arbitrarily chose the left-hand binding posts on each transformer to serve as the common ground and running rail connections.

Once you've linked all the grounds together, plug all the transformer cords into the power strip, plug the strip into a 115-volt wall outlet, and switch it on. Turn all the transformer speed control levers about halfway up. Then connect a wire to the other binding post of the first transformer (the right-hand terminal in the illustration) and gently touch the wire to the same post on the second transformer. If a spark is produced when they touch, reverse the plug on the second transformer by rotating it 180 degrees in the power strip outlet. Touch the second post with the wire again. If no spark appears, you know the second transformer is in phase with the first. Repeat this operation with all the remaining transformers. Your transformers are in phase and ready to go.

Using a Common Ground

I recommend "common ground," or "common return," wiring, regardless of the kind of transformer arrangement or power source you use. My reason is simple: Common ground is a logical system that can simplify your wiring and save money because you'll use only about half as much wire as you would with conventional wiring.

Instead of using two wires to complete each electrical circuit with the transformer, you connect only one to the "hot," "outgoing," or "center rail"

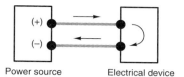

Conventional Circuit

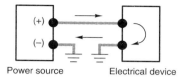

Common-ground Circuit

side of the circuit. The "ground," or "return," side of the circuit uses a path in common with all the other circuits in the system to get back to the power source. One ground connection may be used for all the track blocks, switch motors, lights, and accessories on the layout. It doesn't matter how many circuits share the same common ground, all find their own paths back to the power source without interfering with each other. (Electricity just works that way; don't ask how!)

Large Lionel transformers, particularly those with several control circuits, often have common ground terminals that have been connected internally to simplify wiring. If your transformer does not have these terminals, or if you aren't sure if it does, consult the chart at right. It shows the various circuit combinations available on many of the popular Lionel models and should help you make your selection of a common ground terminal.

Many operators find it convenient to use the track running rails as common ground connections for all the electrical circuits on their layouts. This is an efficient method for small and medium-sized model railroads. On large ones, however, with their long stretches of track and numerous lights and accessories that drain away power, I suggest connecting all the ground circuits to a thick copper wire running underneath. Electricians call such a wire a "bus." (I don't know why; ask them, since they're the ones getting $80.00 an hour!) Ground bus wires usually are installed around the periphery of a layout or cut across it diagonally. That puts them in close proximity to the track and accessory circuits they serve.

Fixed-Voltage Bus Wires

Think of ground and fixed-voltage bus wires as convenient extensions of the binding post terminals on your transformer. That's what they are. They extend the reach of those terminals so you can avoid having a confusing jumble of wires at the control panel.

Transformer	Common or Ground Post	Fixed-Voltage Posts	Variable-Voltage Posts
KW Multi-control	U	D 20 V C 6 V	A 6–20 V B 6–20 V
	C	D 14 V U 6 V	A 0–14 V B 0–14 V
RW Multi-control	A	D 19 V C 9 V	U 9–19 V
	B	D 16 V C 6 V	U 6–16 V
	D	A 19 V B 16 V C 10 V	None
	U	None	A 9–19 V B 6–16 V
V, Z, V220, Z220	U	None	A 6–25 V B 6–25 V C 6–25 V D 6–25 V
VW, ZW Multi-control	U	None	A* 6–20 V B 6–20 V C 6–20 V D* 6–20 V
1032, 1033, 1233, 1032M Multi-control	A	C 16 V B 5 V	U 5–16 V
	B	C 11 V	U 0–11 V
	C	A 16 V B 11 V	None
	U	None	A 5–16 V B 0–11 V
1034	A	C 20 V B 6 V	U 10–20 V
	B	C 14 V A 6 V	U 4–14 V
	C	A 20 V B 14 V	None
	U	None	A 10–20 V B 4–14 V
*With internal whistle control			

Transformer terminals used for common ground wiring.

Unless your layout is very small and uncomplicated, I highly recommend that you install heavy-gauge bus wires underneath it to simplify hooking up the hot sides of your fixed-voltage accessory and lighting circuits. You actually may need two or more such buses with different fixed-voltage outputs to match the requirements of the accessories you intend to operate.

For the layout shown here, I've used only one bus, which carries 14 fixed volts. I made this

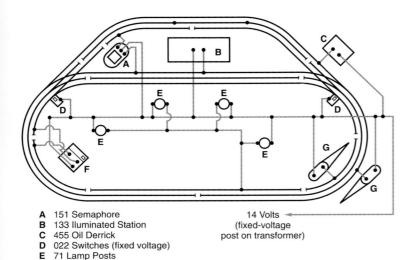

A 151 Semaphore
B 133 Illuminated Station
C 455 Oil Derrick
D 022 Switches (fixed voltage)
E 71 Lamp Posts
F 145 Automatic Gateman
G 252 Crossing Gate

14 Volts
(fixed-voltage
post on transformer)

Fixed-voltage bus accessory wiring using insulated track sections for activation.

compromise for the sake of clarity. The illuminated accessories need less voltage than the animated ones. As you can see, all the circuits are grounded through the running rails of the track. In addition, I used special insulated track sections (described in Chapter 3) instead of contactors to activate the automatic gateman, crossing gates, and semaphore.

If you install them with great care, permanent bus wires may be left bare to make hooking up the accessories easy at almost any spot along the line. Obviously, the bare bus wires shouldn't come in contact with other bare wires, and they should be rigidly fixed to something that doesn't conduct electricity, such as the wood benchwork or the underside of the table top. Holding them with staples, driven in every two feet or so, will keep them in place.

Yes, you should solder these bus wire connections. Specially tinned solid copper wire is available to make the job easier. I know that many otherwise brave people cringe at the idea of soldering things together. Well, the process isn't difficult once you learn how. For those readers who would like to try soldering, I have included a section on basic soldering techniques at the end of this chapter.

If you can't overcome the "solder-phobia," you can try some of these alternative, albeit less satisfactory methods of connecting accessory wires to the bus lines.

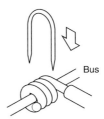

1. Strip about an inch of insulation from the end of the accessory wire. Next, wind it tightly around the bus wire three or four times. Then, position a staple over this connection and hammer it into the wood benchwork as hard as you can. That should keep it in place.

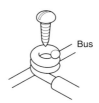

2. Strip about half an inch of insulation from the end of the accessory wire, and loop it around the shaft of a short wood or sheet-metal screw that has a large round head. Drive the screw into the benchwork next to the bus wire. Sometimes putting a washer on the screw helps in making this kind of connection.

Many types of "solderless" lugs and terminals, as well as crimping tools to apply them, are available from hardware and electrical supply stores. You may find these useful items in wiring a layout, though I think it's a long and expensive way of trying to get around learning how to solder two wires together.

Fixed Voltage for Remote Control Track Sections

Using fixed voltage on UCS or 6019 Remote Control Track Sections improves their performance and allows them to function even when track power is off. The conversion is simple, involving only one wire.

To change a UCS track to fixed-voltage operation, first unhook the number 3 wire in the cable (counting from the left) from its terminal on the track section and connect it to a 15-volt accessory bus or directly to a similar post on a transformer.

If you're working with an O27 gauge 6019 Remote Control Track, unhook the number 4 wire in the cable (the one on the extreme right). There are no screw terminals on these sections, so you must unsolder or cut the wires.

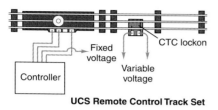

UCS Remote Control Track Set

Because of a shortage of controllers, a lack of space on the control panel, or a wish to eliminate confusion in crowded yards, some operators decide to connect two or more Remote Control Tracks in parallel with each other so they can be operated by one controller. It makes little difference electrically how many tracks you connect in this way because the only one that works when you push the buttons is the track with the train directly over it.

Preserving the Sequence Reverse Mode

The usual procedure when operating trains on block- or cab-controlled layouts using toggle switches is to lock out the E-unit sequence reversing mechanisms and run all locomotives in the "forward only" mode. The scheme recommended by Lionel to preserve the reversing feature of the locomotives, even though insulated blocks are used, is to "jump" the insulating pin going into each block with a 10-ohm, 25-watt adjustable resistor, as shown below.

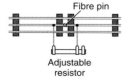

A second and perhaps preferable way to put such a resistor into the circuit would be across the toggle switch terminals, as shown below.

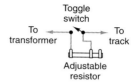

With either installation, you can then adjust the resistor to permit just enough current to leak into the insulated block to keep the reverse unit's solenoid energized, though not enough to operate the locomotive's motor. Making this adjustment can be tricky, but it's worth the effort. You can obtain resistors of this type from industrial electrical or electronics supply companies.

Selecting Wires, Toggle Switches, and Other Electrical Components

As you've probably figured out by now, I am genetically frugal and don't like to spend any more money than I have to in order to get a job done. All the same, this isn't the place to skimp on quality in deference to price. If you've ever wired a layout, you know that it is one of those projects you wouldn't want to do over because you foolishly cut corners the first time.

First, make sure you buy wire that is heavy enough. The point is to have wire with more current-carrying capacity than you'll need. Enough power is wasted by the resistance inherent in tinplate track, so you don't want to lose any more through the wires leading up to it.

Whether you use solid or stranded wire is not as important as having a heavy enough gauge. Consider 12- or 14-gauge for buses and ground returns. Sixteen-gauge wire is the minimum for track feeders. Eighteen- or 20-gauge is adequate for short runs to lights and accessories. Throw out anything smaller than twenty-gauge wire before you start.

Second, purchase an array of different colored wires. Consistent color-coding of circuits makes under-the-table troubleshooting and repair much easier. Pick a particular color for a certain application and stick with it. Use leftovers for short lighting and accessory runs.

Third, toggle switches come in a wide variety of types, sizes, and price ranges. The temptation is great to save a few dollars on switches that appear to be adequate for the job. Don't give in! Even though most train circuits carry only 20 volts at 2 or 3 amps, I always buy the heavy-duty toggles that are designed to carry household power loads of 115 volts at 10 or more amps. By relying on these heavy-duty switches, I can count on their never being overloaded or becoming pitted from excessive arcing. Install good toggle switches, and they'll still be working long after you have retired.

Soldering

I don't think there is any other facet of this hobby fraught with so much anxiety and denial, or overgrown with as many misconceptions, as soldering. There is no good reason for these reactions because soldering is an acquired skill, perfected through practice. No, you may not be good at it the first time you try, but did you expect to bowl 300 or hit a hole in one right away?

I can't remember exactly how or when I learned to solder. In my youth, while working the long night shift at a local radio station, I watched the engineers repair studio equipment. Their soldering iron was always hot, just like the coffee pot. Mainly, I observed, asking only a few questions and not wanting to unmask my ignorance.

Still, one day, I bought a cheap 25-watt iron and tried to do what the engineers did. It was very difficult, because my little iron didn't get hot enough. The solder took forever to flow. Most of my connections were dull or grainy. Then I spotted a 100-watt Wen soldering gun on sale, and that changed my perspective. The gun heated up quickly, and the solder melted like butter. I can't say that I was ever good at soldering, but I managed to make the connections on the first try, at least most of the time.

I kept that Wen gun for thirty years. Its case was cracked from hitting the floor so many times. Glued and held together with friction tape, the thing just kept on working. I must have replaced the tip a couple of dozen times. Then the company went out of business and spare parts were no longer available, so I had to buy another gun. (There' a lesson in this about obsolescence.)

Wanting to treat myself to the best, I invested in a big, dual-range Craftsman, which I never quite got used to. If I squeezed the trigger a little too hard, the thing went into the high range, which was very disconcerting. I'm sure it was my fault, but I swore long and often at the guy who invented such a fickle, unpredictable, hair-triggered monstrosity. Imagine my delight when I found a 100-watt model that felt and handled just like my old gun. I found it at Radio Shack, of all places, and laid in a good supply of new tips before I left the store.

Somewhere along the way I also acquired an Ungar soldering pencil, a low-powered iron with a very thin tip for working on tiny jobs or in tight quarters. There's nothing else like it when you need it, which I have to admit isn't very often.

For what it's worth, here is my soldering arsenal: a big, dual-range blunderbuss that's hardly ever used; a thin soldering pencil that's nothing to write home about; and my workhorse hundred-watter with a pistol grip. Overall, I prefer guns. Some of my friends like irons. It's a personal thing, I guess, whatever you're comfortable with. There certainly is a wide range of soldering equipment available, for every type of job and every level of skill. There even are cordless guns on the market now. (No comment, no experience, no desire to gain any.)

I can't recommend the dual-range guns with a clear conscience, because I never got the hang of using one. They certainly aren't for beginners. I also cringe when I see little 30-watt irons for sale, again based upon my own experiences. I suggest buying something in between and following the manufacturer's instructions regarding its use. I happen to like my gun because I'm used to it; the thing heats quickly, and it can be used on a wide variety of jobs in and around the train room.

If you want to take up soldering, and I strongly advise you to do so if you're serious about the toy train hobby, here are a few guidelines.

1. Buy or borrow a soldering tool (a gun or an iron) and familiarize yourself with how it works.

2. Buy a spool of solder and some paste flux. Use only rosin-core solder and rosin flux for electrical work. The acid-core stuff is for plumbers and sheet-metal workers. It oxidizes and corrodes in time and will ruin any electrical connections made with it. Similarly, don't be confused by the

specialty solders on the market. The standard 60:40 (tin-to-lead ratio) is good for general use. Get solder with a fairly thin diameter because it melts faster. (I noticed for the first time "lead free" solder and couldn't help wondering if the stuff works about as well as the "lead free" paint we're forced to use. No further comment!)

3. Tin your new tool according to the manufacturer's directions. If your gun or iron isn't new, tin it anyway. If it's rough or pitted from use, smooth the tip first with a fine file. Then smear some flux on the tip. Turn on the tool and heat it up. Next, run a bit of solder over the tip. The solder should adhere and look shiny. If it drips down, you used too much.

4. Practice using the gun or iron. Solder scrap wires and metal pieces together until you get the hang of the process. Practice some more.

5. Clean the surfaces of whatever you intend to solder. They have to be free of rust, corrosion, oxidation, dirt, and grease. I use fine emery paper for this, even on new materials.

6. Smear flux on the areas where you want the solder to flow and adhere.

7. If possible, make a good mechanical connection first. Twist wires together as tightly as possible. Don't rely on the solder to form the connection by itself.

8. Heat the work with your soldering tool. Remember to apply the solder to the work itself and not to the tool.

9. Touch the heated work with the solder. Let the solder flow until you think there's enough to hold the connection firmly.

10. Lift the soldering tool away from the work, but don't disturb the work itself until you're sure the solder has hardened. You usually can see it change from a liquid to a solid state. It takes only a few seconds.

11. If you don't get everything done right the first time, reheat the connection. Solder in its liquid state is smooth and shiny. As it hardens, the shiny luster tones down slightly, but the overall appearance remains smooth and bright. If your finished work is dull, wrinkled, or grainy, you have what is known as a "cold solder joint," or a "rosin connection," which will give you trouble in the future. So reheat the work until the solder flows again, add a bit more solder if necessary, and wait for it to harden. Repeat this until you're satisfied with the result.

12. (There always have to be twelve steps in a program, right?) Be careful as you work. Don't touch the iron. Be sure to watch out for excess solder dripping from the work. It is molten metal and particularly hard on human skin and polyester clothing.

What about covering your newly soldered connection? Good old electrician's tape still works well. Wind the stuff around the wires like a bandage. But heat-shrink tubing makes a better, more professional-looking job. It comes in a number of different diameters and can be slipped over your wires before you connect them. When you've finished, slip the tubing over the joint. The heat from a match or cigarette lighter shrinks the tubing around the connection, giving it a continuous and tight-fitting covering.

III. CLASSIC TOY TRAIN TECHNOLOGY

Chapter Nine

BASIC MECHANICS FOR TOY TRAIN TINKERERS

I have long stood in awe of the inventive genius of those individuals who worked in the engineering departments of Lionel, Gilbert, and Marx. It's amazing how they were able to scale down the essential principles of physics and mechanics to the size of the trains they produced and create wondrous toys that often aspired to the level of kitsch masterpieces in the way that they, not always flawlessly, imitated life. But what in life is flawless anyway? So, in that respect too, their creations were microcosms of the real world, warts and all.

To understand how these charming miniature marvels worked, or were intended to work, we must explore the realm of the mechanical—of gears, levers, pulleys, and shafts—in at least enough depth to comprehend how all the widgets and gadgets interacted with each other. This chapter strives to do just that so you can communicate with the people who repair electric trains.

Gears

The most common type of gears are known as "spur gears." They're basically toothed wheels that mesh with each other and transfer synchronized rotation from one shaft to one or more other shafts that lie parallel to it. Mechanics call two or more gears functioning together a "gear train."

When only two spur gears are used in a gear train, their rotation will be in opposite directions, as shown below.

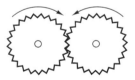

Therefore, to achieve rotation in the same direction, you have to insert a third gear, known as an "idler," or "intermediate," between the original two gears. As shown below, the idler need not be

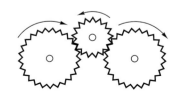

of the same diameter as the other two gears as long as its teeth match with theirs.

These principles may be applied to any number of geared shafts within a gear train.

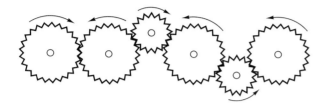

The relative diameters of the gears in a gear train affect the speed of shaft rotation. To increase or reduce the speed of shaft rotation, you can vary the gear sizes accordingly. This principle is known as "gear reduction." The shaft with the smaller gear spins faster, as shown below.

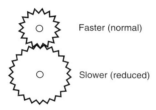

To achieve a "double reduction," a mechanic would mount a large and a small gear on the same shaft. These are known as "cluster gears."

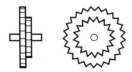

Often, though not always, cluster gears serve as idlers in a gear train, as shown in the gear train used in a typical Lionel steam locomotive.

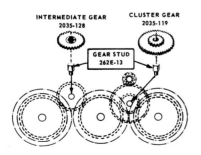

These principles may be applied to any number of geared shafts within a gear train. Clock makers have used multiple gear reductions for centuries.

A "rack and pinion" is a device created to translate reciprocating motion into rotary motion or vice versa. The rack is essentially a number of geared teeth on a straight bar instead of a round wheel. The pinion is a spur gear that meshes with the teeth on the rack at a 90 degree angle. The action of the pinion is limited by the length of the rack, as shown below.

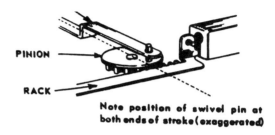

Note position of swivel pin at both ends of stroke (exaggerated)

A rack and pinion is used to throw the swivel rails on Lionel's 1122 track switches.

A "worm and wheel" operates at a 90 degree angle to each other, translating rotary motion, which usually is reduced at the same time. Instead of teeth, the worm has spiral threads, similar to those on a screw. The teeth on the worm wheel are cut at an angle to match the pitch of the worm threads. So, as the worm turns, so does the wheel, but usually at a lower rate of speed, as is shown below:

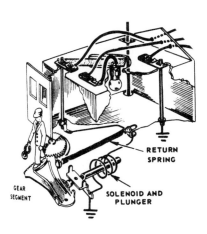

A curved rack under the figure of the 145 automatic gateman caused the large pinion to rotate, opening the door of the shanty.

There are many other gear types, with infinite variations in the world of machinery. However, the gears I've described are the ones most often encountered with toy trains.

New gears mesh tightly with each other, turning quietly on the slightly rounded (convex) side walls of their teeth. As the gears wear, the mesh becomes looser, and then they start to make a clattering noise. Eventually, the teeth wear out or break off and the meshing ceases completely. Keeping them lightly greased retards the wear process dramatically.

Pulleys, Sprockets, Belts, and Chains

Mechanics often use these ominous-sounding devices in the same way as they do gears: to drive two or more parallel shafts, though in applications where the use of gearing may be unnecessary or impractical. For example, when the shafts are spaced far apart, two "sprockets" with an "endless chain" loop between them may be more practical than a long train of gears, as is shown below.

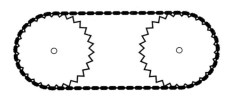

By the same token, if a design doesn't require synchronization between the shafts, a simple "pulley-and-belt" arrangement may suffice, as shown below:

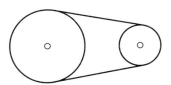

As with gear trains, a difference in relative sprocket or pulley size produces a difference in shaft rotation speed. During the prewar era, engineers at Lionel used the sprocket and chain idea on several accessories. By contrast, a number of operating cars and accessories developed in the postwar period relied on pulleys.

Bearings: Bushings, Balls, and Needles

A "bearing" is the contact area that bears the load; it is the part in which shafts, pivots, and the like turn or move. Mechanics use bearings to minimize friction and/or to distribute force in a way that will reduce wear. A "journal" is the part of a shaft that comes in contact with a bearing.

"Bushings" are the simplest types of bearings. Usually replaceable, they form a lining for a hole in the machinery in order to protect it from abrasion and wear.

Lionel's engineers commonly used axle bushings on the firm's spur-geared steam locomotive mechanisms. Without these parts, the thin side plates would soon wear out from the driver axle rotation.

"Ball bearings" should be familiar to anyone who has ever owned a bicycle. They are small steel spheres used to minimize friction between two metal surfaces that come in moving contact with each other.

A "thrust bearing" usually is a single ball bearing that rides within a sleeve or cap at the end of a shaft. The reason for such a design is that friction will be lessened if the shaft turns upon and/or pushes against one tiny area on the surface of a sphere at any given time.

Lionel used single thrust bearings at the ends of whistle armature shafts and in small motorized units, such as the gang car and trolley.

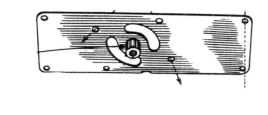

Lionel often used a ball bearing inside a bushing as a thrust bearing for an armature shaft, such as this one from a whistle motor.

Generally speaking, a "race" is a round fixture in which a number of ball bearings are held. Remember your bike wheels? Several ball bearings positioned around a shaft will reduce friction, just as adding a single thrust bearing at the end of the shaft would do. Lionel used races of ball bearings around the armature shafts of its heavy-duty motors.

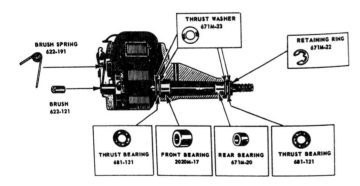

Two races of ball bearings were used as thrust bearings on many of Lionel's heavy-duty motors.

"Needle bearings" operate on the same principle as ball bearings: the smaller the mass of a moving shaft that comes in contact with a journal, the less friction there will be. Designers bevel the shaft to a small and rounded tip, which is the only surface that rides within the journal.

For half a century, scale model railroaders have used needle-bearing trucks to reduce drag and facilitate longer trains. Unfortunately, when Lionel began making such trucks in the 1970s, the company called them "needlepoint bearings," which must have been confusing to artists and embroiderers.

> **NEEDLEPOINT BEARINGS**
> Lionel needlepoint bearings provide free-wheeling action through virtually friction-free bearing operation. This means more cars can be pulled than ever before. This allows longer trains.

Needle, or "needlepoint," bearings were used in Lionel's truck journals after 1970 to reduce friction and facilitate longer trains.

Pistons, Cylinders, and Dash Pots

The "piston-and-cylinder" principle is familiar to almost everyone, thanks in large part to the automobile engine. A round, cylindrical "piston" moves up and down within a hollow tube, or "cylinder," with a slightly larger circumference.

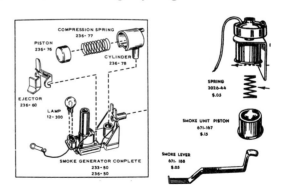

Pistons and cylinders can be found in both types of Lionel smoke units.

Lionel relied on this principle to produce the puffing effect of the smoke in its steam engines. The rotation of the driving wheels activated a crank or cam, which caused the piston to move up and down within the cylinder. The upward stroke of the piston sent a puff of air through a small hole in the head of the cylinder, into the smoke generating chamber, and out the stack. There were a number of variations in the mechanical parts over the years, but the basic idea remained the same.

A "dash pot" typically consists of a piston and cylinder that have been machined to very close tolerances. A viscous liquid, usually a thick, petroleum-based lubricant, is added to form a pneumatic seal between the piston and the cylinder wall. This oil seal does not prevent the piston from moving, but does retard its action.

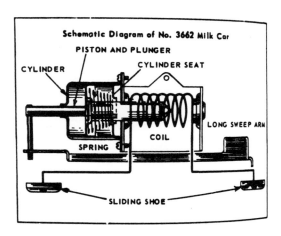

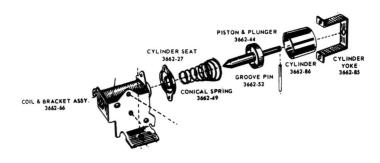

Starting in 1955, Lionel used a dash pot on the modified design of its milk car. The piston was attached to a solenoid plunger.

Lionel used dash pots to slow down the movement of some operating cars and accessories. The most notable example is the redesigned mechanism installed in the operating milk car. This improvement changed the little figure that delivered the cans of milk. Now the man slowly delivered each can and carefully placed it on the platform, instead of acting as though a bull inside the car was chasing him.

Arms, Levers, and Cranks

Distinguishing between an "arm" and a "lever" can be difficult. After all, all levers have arms, but not all arms are necessarily part of a lever. It all depends upon the application.

Levers tend to be rigid pieces that rotate upon a fixed axis, or support, called a "fulcrum." Two opposing forces are operational with levers: "applied force" and "resisting force." Generally speaking, the longer the arm on the applied force side of the fulcrum, the more resisting force the lever can handle.

A "crank" usually is nothing more than an arm that projects at a right angle to an axis or shaft, which receives or imparts motion. As the illustration indicates, cranks are used to communicate motion and change rotary motion into reciprocating motion or vice versa.

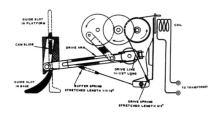

Many Lionel accessories were ingenious combinations of mechanical and electrical components. The 264 fork lift platform, for example, had triple-reduction gearing, levers, arms, pivots, swivels, cams, and springs, all of which were connected to a vibration motor.

Pivots and Swivels

A "pivot" is the point upon which something hinges, rotates, or oscillates. Engineers often design the end of a pin or shaft to serve as a pivot and turn within a bearing.

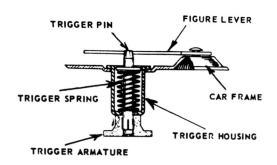

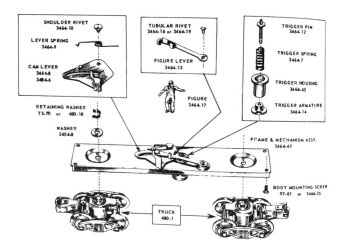

Lionel's operating boxcars were fascinating combinations of springs, cams, levers, and pivots. A locking mechanism made them work.

Mechanics sometimes use the word "swivel" interchangeably with "pivot." However, a swivel can be part of a pivot. It is a fastening device that allows whatever is attached to it to turn freely upon it. Get the difference?

Cams and Eccentrics

Here are two more terms that are confusing to many people, particularly some of my relatives. A "cam" is an irregularly shaped piece or wheel, commonly elliptical or heart-shaped, that's fastened to and revolves with a shaft. The cam engages with another mechanism, known as a "cam follower," to convert regular rotary motion into irregular or reciprocating motion, as shown at the top of the right-hand column on this page.

An "eccentric," on the other hand, is a rotating axis that is off center from the axis of the main rotating shaft. It converts circular motion into

Cams on steam locomotive drivers or axles were used to create the regular puffing effect of the smoke as synchronized with the rotation of the drivers. In this illustration, the cam, which controlled the smoke lever, was cast into the interior of one of the spur gears.

reciprocating or rectilinear (straight line) motion without the use of a cam follower or another similar mechanism.

I won't mention "eccentric cranks"; doing so might get too close to a few of those farther up in my family tree.

Springs

Springs have two elementary designs that can create many variations: the "flat," or "leaf," type and the "coil," or "wound," type. They're made of a resilient material, usually specially treated steel or wire.

Engineers use springs for many purposes: to drive a mechanism, as in the mainspring of a clock or watch; to apply or relieve pressure; and to serve as a cushion or simple return device. Lionel's designers loved springs and found hundreds of highly creative uses for all types and sizes of springs over the years.

Springs sometimes lose their resiliency. This is particularly true if they've been subjected to repeated heating and cooling or have been stored in a compressed or an extended position for a long time.

Ratchets and Pawls

A "ratchet wheel" resembles a gear, except that the teeth on its edge usually are angled sharply in one direction. A "pawl" is a pivoted bar that's designed to engage with the ratchet-wheel teeth to convert reciprocating motion into rotary motion or to prevent reversal of the wheel by locking it in place.

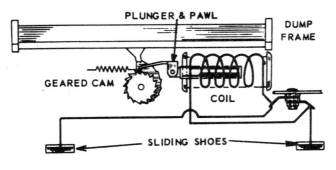

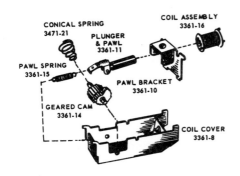

A ratchet and pawl, on the same axis with a geared cam, made the dump frame move upward on the 3361 lumber car.

Engineers at Lionel installed ratchets and pawls in a number of its operating cars and accessories. However, the company's most common use was as part of the three-position E-unit sequence reverse mechanism that came on most of the locomotives it produced over more than half a century.

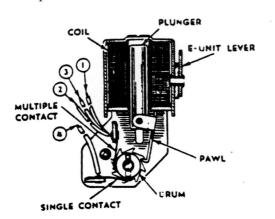

A pawl attached to the solenoid plunger engaged the ratchet that was molded into the drum of an E-unit. This caused it to rotate one position every time power was interrupted.

Nuts, Bolts, Rivets, and Screws

Trends in manufacturing methods over the years are mirrored by toy train production and are dramatically reflected in the choice of fasteners used to keep the parts together. In the early years of mass-produced toy trains, machine screws in tapped holes were common, along with nuts, bolts, and washers in soldered or spot-welded subassemblies. The idea was to make durable products that were easy to take apart for service (or to just take apart).

In the 1940s, when injection-molded plastics began to replace die-cast and sheet-metal construction, production methods also changed to become faster and less labor intensive. Designers used more rivets in place of nut-bolt-washer assemblies. They made sheet-metal screws, especially the self-tapping kind, the norm. When they relied on conventional screws, they specified the kind capped with speed nuts. Sometimes, designers even had parts glued together. The era of easy assembly superseded the era of easy service.

"Screws" are designed to be turned into threaded holes for the purpose of joining two or more objects. They come in a wide variety of sizes, lengths, and head styles. Four types of heads are often found in train repair, each of which requires its own type of screwdriver.

Common Phillips Hexagon Set

There are seven head shapes, along with the headless set screw. Each of them has a different application:

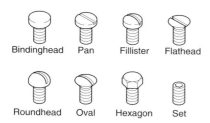

A screw's descriptive nomenclature tells its diameter expressed as a numerical size, length in inches, the number of threads per inch, and type of head. For example, as shown below, 2-56 x ¼F describes a size 2 screw that has 56 threads per inch, measures ¼ inch long, and comes with a Fillister head.

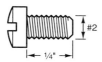

Some screws have threads that don't reach all the way to the head, These are known as "lag," or "shouldered," screws. Another kind that's widely used is the "self-tapping" screw. As shown below, it "taps," or "threads," a hole as it is driven into a material. You can recognize self-tapping screws by their tapered profiles and the grooves cut through the threads at their ends (to give them a crescent-shaped cross-section).

Sheet-metal screws (shown below) are designed to join two or more thin sheets of metal. They also are tapered, but their threads are spaced farther apart than is true with a conventional screw. In many ways, they resemble wood screws, but their threads go all the way to their heads.

"Bolts" are essentially the same as screws, except that they're intended for insertion through threaded nuts instead of tapped holes. "Nuts" come in the same numerical sizes as screws and, as shown below, usually are hexagonal or square in shape.

Top to bottom: two kinds of nuts, three lock washers, and a speed nut.

"Washers" are sized to fit their bolt and nut combinations. Thin and usually round, they're placed under bolt heads and ahead of nuts. "Lock washers," which tend to be made of steel, are intended to lock together a bolt-and-nut assembly by digging into the surfaces of the joined pieces. They come in three types, two of which have serrated interior or exterior edges. The third kind of lock washer, which is made of spring steel, doesn't form a perfect circle.

"Speed nuts" are a relatively recent invention. Made of springy sheet steel, they're forced over the screw threads by a machine. Once pressed into place, they serve the same functions as a conventional nut and a lock washer combined (at least that's the theory).

Left to right: common rivet, hollow rivet, shouldered rivet, eyelet rivet, and split rivet.

"Common rivets" are solid metal cylinders with unslotted heads that are designed to join two or more pieces. You insert them through holes in the work and then flatten their protruding ends, usually with a hammer or machine.

"Hollow rivets" are tubular cylinders with unslotted heads that mechanics use in the same way as they do common rivets. However, hollow rivets are intended to be flared out with a special riveting tool or punch.

"Shouldered rivets" are used in applications where permanently joined pieces require some freedom of movement and must not be fixed in one position.

"Eyelet rivets" tend to be short, hollow rivets that have holes in their heads. When one is inserted through a hole in the work and fastened into place, a usable hole remains, but in a smaller diameter.

"Split rivets" are hardware store items that have no real industrial applications. Handymen use them to replace the more conventional rivets.

Chapter Ten

ELECTRICAL COMPONENTS BEFORE THE ELECTRONIC AGE

To benefit from this section on the electrical side of toy train technology, you'll probably need a basic understanding of how electricity and electrical currents work and a familiarity with some of the terminology involved. This knowledge should help you interpret wiring diagrams and troubleshoot problems with your trains and accessories as they arise.

Let's begin with the two types of electrical currents. The first, known as "direct current" (DC), features a relatively steady flow of current in only one direction, which is usually expressed as flowing from "positive" (+) to "negative" (-) in a circuit. The second type, known as "alternating current" (AC), differs in that its flow of current rapidly alternates in direction many times every second (+ to -, - to +, + to -, - to +). We express the speed of this alternation in "cycles per second," a unit of measurement known as hertz (Hz).

Most of the electric power distributed in the United States is alternating current, with a frequency of 60 cycles per second (60 Hz). Most household electrical appliances and devices, including O gauge electric trains, are designed to operate on this type of power.

Direct current is generally used for trains in other scales, such as HO, N, and G. Some of the "rock-bottom economy line" Lionel O gauge trains produced in the 1970s and 1980s also used DC. To operate, they require "power packs," which change AC into DC, or storage batteries, all of which are DC.

Transformers and power packs serve, above all, to reduce the relatively dangerous 115-volt electric power that comes from wall outlets to a lower, safer level, usually less than 20 volts, that can be fed into the track. Their secondary function involves regulating the flow of that reduced power.

Comparison to the Flow of Water

People often compare the flow of electricity to the flow of water. Admittedly, this analogy can be helpful in promoting understanding of elementary electrical currents, but it breaks down after that. However, for the sake of initial clarity, you may consider the electricity to be water, the transformer to serve as a pump, and the wires to act as pipes.

Continuing in this vein, we have an unlimited supply of water (electricity) at our disposal, though our pump (the transformer) is capable of moving only a certain amount of it in a given time. (In electrical terms, this capacity is expressed as a "wattage rating.") The more water (electricity) that has to be moved, the higher the capacity of the pump (the wattage rating of the transformer) needs to be.

Similarly, the diameter of the pipe determines how much water can be forced to flow through it. The larger its diameter, the more water a pipe will handle without bursting. There is a direct correlation here with the size of an electrical wire: The thicker the wire, the more electricity it can handle without burning up. We measure a pipe's diameter in inches and the thickness of wire according to its gauge number. The lower the gauge number, the thicker the wire. Why? I don't know. (Go ask Benjamin Franklin or Thomas Edison!)

For the sake of furthering the analogy, you may consider the diameter of the pipe (the thickness of the wire) as an indication of the flow capacity of the system. (In electrical terms, this is expressed as "amperage.") The pressure of the water in the system is analogous to the force of the electricity (expressed as "voltage").

You can compare the rheostat throttle on a transformer to a faucet; you can shut it off completely, allow a little to trickle or dribble, or open it up wide and allow the full force of the water (electricity) to flow through the system. The more the rheostat, like a faucet, is turned up, the less resistance there is to the flow. We measure resistance in electricity in "ohms."

Electrical Circuits

As electrical current flows, it makes a loop that we call a "circuit." The circuit begins at the power source, where current leaves through one of the two wires that connect that source with the device to be electrified. Then the current enters the motor, light bulb, or other device, only to return to the power source via the second wire. We refer to the outgoing part of the circuit as the "hot," or (+) side, and the return part as the "ground" or (-) side. You must complete the circuit in order for the electrical device to function. In terms of Lionel's trains, you should think of the center rail as (+) and the outside ones as (-).

You can intentionally interrupt the flow of current moving through a circuit by a switch on the (+) side, the (-) side, or both sides of an electrical device. Doing so will shut it off. We call a switch that interrupts only one side of a circuit "single-pole" and one that interrupts both sides "double-pole." Some switches interrupt, or "break," a circuit that normally is closed; others complete, or "make" a normally open circuit.

With a "short circuit," the flow of current takes a short cut to return to the power source before traversing the entire loop, thereby bypassing the electrical device it was intended to power. The energy that the electrical device should have expended still exists in the now-shortened loop, but now it has no place to go. Consequently, it gets frustrated and turns into heat.

Well, our first lesson in toy train electronics has ended, and it really wasn't as difficult as you expected. You now have the rudiments of electrical theory as well as all the relevant terms (AC, DC, Hz, amps, ohms, volts, and watts), with each explained in as much depth as you'll likely ever need to know. Now we're ready to see how designers applied some of these basic principles in the engineering of vintage toy trains.

Electromagnets

An electromagnet is simply an iron core with a coil of wire wrapped around it. As electricity is sent through the coil, the electromagnet either attracts or repels other ferrous metals. When the electricity is turned off, the flow of magnetic energy, known as "flux," ceases. The direction of the flux, whether the electromagnet attracts or repels, is a function of the way in which the coil is wrapped around the iron core.

The strength of the magnetism, or "flux density," is determined by the size of the core as well as the size of the wire used and/or the number of windings in the coil. Generally speaking, the larger the core surface and the more windings on it, the more powerful the magnet.

Lionel used electromagnets in the UCS, 6019, and subsequent uncoupling tracks. Its designers also relied on electromagnets in such accessories as the 165 and 182 magnetic cranes, 282 portal gantry crane, and the various reissues of the 282 brought out in the last fifteen years.

If you discover an electromagnet isn't operating, check first for a broken lead wire and repair it.

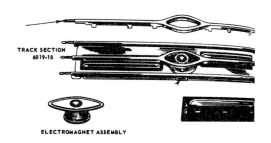

Electromagnets were used in Remote Control Track Sections to activate Lionel's knuckle couplers.

Or the coil itself may be burned out. If so, the best course is to replace it; coil winding is an advanced skill far beyond the technical scope of this book.

Relays

A relay is nothing more than an electromagnet that has a movable iron armature attached to it, usually by a pivot at one end. One or more electrical contacts are attached to the pivoting armature. Whenever the electromagnet is energized, the armature is attracted to it, and the contacts either make or break their electrical circuits. As the electromagnet is shut off, the armature returns to its normal, rest position, usually by spring pressure or the force of gravity.

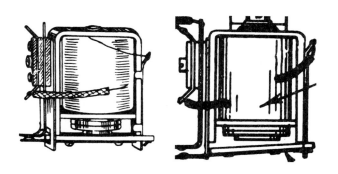

The DC relay used to operate Lionel's whistles and horns is shown with the contacts closed (left) and open (right).

The most common relays encountered in the toy train world are those used to activate Lionel's built-in whistles and horns. They are extremely reliable units and rarely require maintenance beyond occasional contact cleaning. However, sometimes more serious problems appear.

If a relay doesn't operate, check for a broken lead wire or a burned-out coil and repair or replace as indicated.

If a relay sticks, simply adjust the flat pivot spring by bending it slightly until the action resumes and the armature returns easily to its normal, rest position.

If a relay chatters, adjust the pivot spring and/or armature guides until the chattering ceases.

Finally, if intermittent contact or excessive arcing occurs at contacts (visible blue sparks), clean contacts with your trusty TV Tuner Cleaner, followed by fine emery paper if necessary. Adjust contacts by bending them until the arcing has been minimized.

Solenoids

A solenoid is a close cousin to the electromagnet. The main difference is that on a solenoid the coil is wrapped around a hollow, non-magnetic tube and the iron core is movable within that tube. Mechanics usually refer to this movable core as the "plunger," or the "armature."

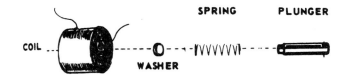

This exploded view of a solenoid shows its basic components: coil, spring, and plunger.

When electricity is sent through the coil, the plunger will move in either direction, depending on how the coil has been wound. Typically, solenoids are set up so that gravity or a spring returns the plunger to its normal, rest position when the electricity is turned off.

You also can create a "double solenoid," which has two coils of wire wound in opposition to each other around the same tube. Selectively energizing one coil or the other can make the plunger move in both directions.

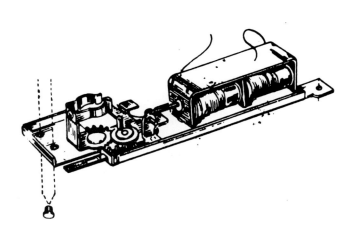

A double solenoid is used to control the swivel rails of an automatic track switch.

Lionel's engineers used the single solenoid principle for the two- and three-position reversing mechanisms that they built into most locomotives produced anywhere from the early 1930s to the advent of electronic directional sequencing just a few years ago. They also relied on single solenoids to activate automatic couplers at one time. As for the double solenoid principle, it was used to selectively change the position of the swivel rails on all varieties of Lionel's automatic track switches.

In addition, Lionel depended on solenoids to operate a mechanical linkage of some sort to provide the action in many of its finest postwar freight cars and accessories. Among the long list of items using solenoids are the 30 and 138 water tanks, 45 and 145 automatic gatemen, 97 coal elevator, 151 semaphore, 152 and 252 automatic crossing gates, 164 log loader, 165 and 182 magnetic cranes, 175 rocket launcher, 262 highway crossing gate, 282 portal gantry crane, 352 ice depot, 415 diesel fueling station, 445 operating switch tower, 455 oil derrick and pump, 497 coaling station, 1045 operating watchman, 3359 twin-bin dump car, 3424 operating brakeman car, 3451 and 3461 operating lumber cars, 3454 and 3854 automatic merchandise cars, 3459 and 3469 ore dump cars, 3462 and 3662 automatic refrigerated milk cars, and 3559 coal dump car.

Here are some tips to remember if you have problems with a solenoid.

- If a solenoid doesn't function, check first for a broken lead wire or a burned-out coil. Repair the wire, or replace the coil. Some parts dealers stock the more common solenoid coils. Again, however, bear in mind that coil winding is an advanced skill far beyond the technical scope of this book.
- Sluggish operation demands that you first check for dirt in the tube or on the plunger. Spray TV Tuner Cleaner directly into the tube, or take out the plunger and soak it in a solvent, such as alcohol or mineral spirits. Clean the tube with the same stuff on a cotton swab.
- If the tube has become distorted because of mishandling or overheating, replacement usually is the only remedy. Never lubricate a solenoid with oil-based products. In extreme cases, you can try powdered graphite or Teflon. Usually, a simple cleaning is enough.

Vibration Motors

Known as "Vibrator Coil Motors," or "Vibrotors," these motors are based on the electromagnetic principle and the fact that most of the electrical energy supplied by power companies in America is alternating current, which oscillates (flows back and forth) at 60 cycles per second. This means a break in the current occurs every $\frac{1}{60}$ second. While this oscillation or interruption happens too fast to be perceived by human senses, we can harness and use it in electrical circuitry.

Although they assume many different shapes and forms in Lionel's operating cars and accessories, all vibration motors operate on the same principle. These motors consist of a simple electromagnet and an iron armature that's mounted in such a way as to keep them separated by a short distance.

When current runs through the electromagnetic coil, the armature is attracted to it yet can't make permanent, intimate contact. Because the electrical current causing the magnetic attraction is interrupted 60 times a second, the armature is alternately pulled toward the magnet and then allowed to return to its normal, rest position each time. This adds up to 120 movements per second, which is so rapid that people perceive it as a continuous vibration. That vibration is the driving force that propels whatever mechanical action has been built into a car or accessory. Three basic types of vibration motors are widely used. We can categorize them according to mechanical function because the electromagnetic principles are the same.

The first type of vibration motor resembles a solenoid in appearance. The coil is wrapped around a hollow tube. The armature, which fits inside the tube, is rigidly mounted to a vibrating structure, such as a platform or ramp. The most common accessories with this kind of vibration motor are the 356 operating freight station, 3356 operating horse car and corral, 3366 circus car and corral, and 3656 stock car and cattle pen. With these accessories, the up-and-down vibration of the platform and/or ramp causes specially designed baggage carts, horses, or cows, respectively, to move around within channels on the surface.

The 362 barrel loader and 3562 barrel car function in the same way. Specially designed barrels move up a ramp, but the vibration creates a side-to-side motion.

The armature used on the barrel loader and the barrel car is flat, not cylindrical, and does not fit within the coil.

The second type, commonly known as the Vibrotor, creates a clockwise rotation around a point located at the center of the coil. The round or cup-shaped armature is free to move in a circular pattern; a rubber drive washer cemented to the armature translates the up-and-down vibration into circular rotation. Little slanted "fingers" molded into the drive washer advance the rotation of the armature by a small fraction of a turn with each vibration cycle.

Among the more common accessories that use this type of vibration motor are the 140 automatic banjo signal, 155 ringing signal, 192 railroad control tower, 197 rotating radar antenna, and 494 rotary beacon. Operating cars that rely on this type

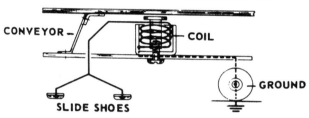

The first type of vibration motor was also used on the 3562 barrel car. This illustration shows how that motor powered the conveyor, which carried the barrels to the end of the car.

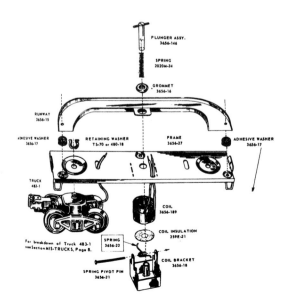

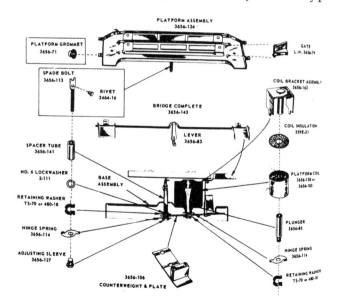

Lionel used the first type of vibration motor on the 3656 cattle car. The exploded view on the left shows how the motor was connected to the runway inside the car. The motor moves the cows because of the "fingers" molded to the bottom of each animal. The view above shows the platform that came with the car. The same type of motor was installed under the platform to keep the cows moving.

of motor include the 3520 and 3620 rotating searchlight cars and 3535 operating security car.

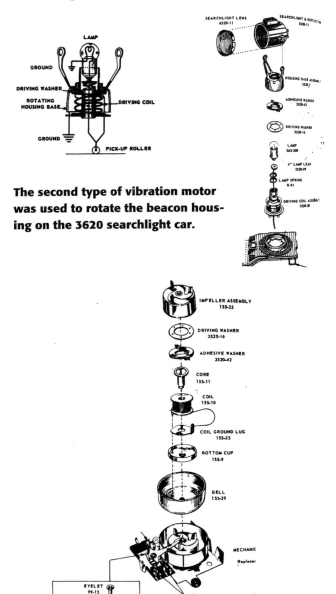

The second type of vibration motor was used to rotate the beacon housing on the 3620 searchlight car.

This exploded view shows how a Vibrotor drives the impeller that trips the bell hammer on a 155 ringing signal.

The third type of vibrating motor has the most complex mechanical linkages attached to it and is sometimes required to perform a number of functions and/or motions at the same time. A spring-loaded drive line translates the linear motion of the armature into rotary motion. This drive line is clamped to the armature and looped around a pulley; at the other end, it is connected to a solid portion of the accessory frame by means of a small tension spring.

When the coil is energized, the armature is attracted to it and snubs the line on the pulley, rotating it a small fraction of a turn. As the current is interrupted, the armature springs back to its normal, rest position and the line slackens. A tension spring then takes up the slack. Because this spring is relatively weak, the line slips back around the pulley without turning it. Therefore, each current pulsation produces a slight motion of the pulley wheel and whatever mechanical apparatus is connected to it.

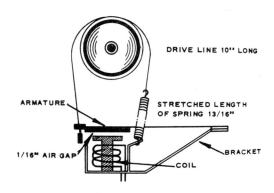

Here is the third type of vibration motor, with its drive lines and pulley arrangement.

This kind of vibrating motor is found on many of Lionel's accessories and operating freight cars from the late 1950s and early 1960s. These include the 128 animated newsstand, 175 rocket launcher, 264 operating fork lift platform, 334 operating dispatching board, 342 culvert pipe loader, 345 culvert pipe unloader, 464 lumber mill, 3435 traveling aquarium, and 3444 animated gondola.

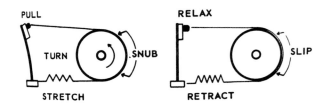

This drawing shows how the "snub and release" action on the drive line makes the pulley turn on the third type of vibration motor.

For servicing and repairing Lionel vibrating motors, here are a couple of guidelines that apply to all three types.

• In case of a dead, nonfunctioning motor (no vibration or humming), begin by checking for a broken lead wire or a burned-out coil. Repair or replace as indicated. Some coils still are available from parts dealers.

• A loud metallic clattering or a buzzing sound means that the air gap between the armature and the coil is not large enough and is causing these parts to rub against each other: Adjust the armature accordingly by bending it.

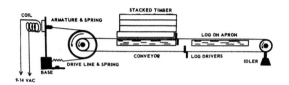

The third type of vibration motor drives the conveyor belt on a 464 lumber mill.

Further problems require you to deal specifically with the type of motor installed on the car or accessory that isn't operating. All models with the first type, with the exception of the barrel loader and barrel car, have an adjustment screw. Turn it until you achieve maximum vibration at the lowest voltage. You can adjust the barrel loader and barrel car by bending the armature arm to get the same result. Also, some ramps and platforms rest on foam rubber pads that can harden over time. Replacing these parts usually improves performance.

Poor performance of items with the second type of vibrating motor tends to be caused by hardened or worn rubber drive washers. Obtain a replacement and secure it in place with contact cement (Goo, available from Wm. K. Walthers, is a good brand). Be sure to keep all interior surfaces and moving parts clean. If, as a last resort, you decide to lubricate the item, use only powdered graphite or Teflon.

Finally, for problems with Lionel cars and accessories that have the third type of motor, start by adjusting the air gap for maximum vibration at the lowest voltage. Then check the condition of the return spring to assure the proper "snub-and-release" action on the pulley. You can make fine adjustments by bending the return-spring mount with pliers. Replace the spring if needed. Should replacement drive line be unavailable, you can substitute unwaxed, 12-pound test braided nylon fishing line.

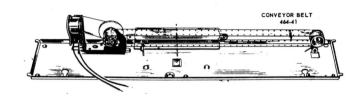

Here's the same motor as installed on the chassis of a 464. Note the perforated conveyor belt on sprocket wheels that's driven by the motor pulley.

Universal Motors

Engineers at Lionel developed its famed AC-DC "universal motor" when many households in rural America still lacked regular power utilities. This motor, which could be used with almost any kind of power source at hand (alternating current, direct current, home generator, or storage batteries), became the mainstay at Lionel. It was durable and reliable, even under heavy use, and required little maintenance or attention except for regular lubrication. When repairs were necessary, common household tools and only a modicum of skill were necessary. Designers used the universal motor in most of Lionel's steam and diesel locomotives until the recent advent of new technology based on can motors and circuit boards.

The universal motor has three basic components. First, there's a stationary field. This stack of thin steel plates, shaped like a horseshoe, is surrounded by many turns of enamel-coated copper wire that mechanics call the "field coil." Next comes a three-pole armature, which consists of a stack of pinwheel-shaped steel plates mounted on a transverse shaft. Three separate coils of enamel-coated wire are wound around the stack in three positions. Each terminates in a "pole piece," a wedge-shaped copper segment on the face of the armature. Together, the three pole pieces form a circle, called the "commutator," that spins around within the stationary field. Third is a pair of copper-graphite brushes, little cylinders that contact the surface of the commutator. They're held firmly in place within individual "brush wells" by spring pressure.

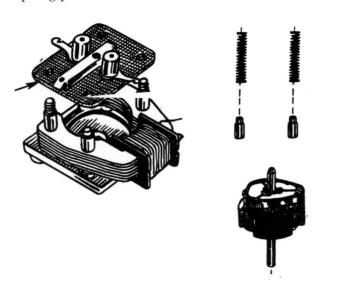

This exploded view of a Lionel universal motor shows its major components: field and brush plate (left) and brush springs, brushes, and armature (right).

When electricity flows into the field coil, the field turns into an electromagnet, the ends of which attract and repel simultaneously. Because of the field's horseshoe shape, these "attract and repel" forces are focused close together. The brushes are wired in series with the field, so electrical current flows through them and into the armature at the same time as the field coil is energized.

The attract and repel forces present at the ends of the field make the armature revolve on its axis. The armature coil that is positioned directly between the ends of the field is forced to move out of the way. As it does, another coil automatically moves into the same position. It, too, must move out of the way, so the third coil takes its place. Then the first one comes back into position again. This cycle continues as long as current flows through the motor.

The armature spins quite rapidly. A typical toy train motor can develop as many as 4,000 rpm. Obviously, this motion must be geared down considerably before it can be practically applied. Regulating the speed of the universal motor involves nothing more than adjusting the input voltage. Reversing the direction of the armature's rotation generally means just switching the wires leading to the brushes.

You must keep the armature shaft bearings lubricated to prevent overheating and minimize bearing wear. Apply one drop of oil after every hour or two of operation, not to mention long periods of storage. Be careful, however, that you don't apply too much lubricant.

In addition, the surface of the commutator has to be kept clean. A dirty commutator is the most common cause of sluggish or erratic operation and excess arcing, which can drastically shorten motor life. A mix of copper-graphite brush residue, spilled lubricant, and dust from the air tends to accumulate on the commutator. You usually can remove it without taking the motor apart by spraying the face of the commutator with TV Tuner Cleaner or rubbing it with cotton swabs dipped in a solvent, such as mineral spirits or alcohol. While you're at it, use a toothpick to clean out the three slots between the pole pieces.

Of course, sometimes things take a more serious turn, and you may discover that you have a dead or inoperative motor on your hands. That kind of problem tends to be a symptom of something being wrong elsewhere, such as in the sequence-reverse mechanism (E-unit). If the motor is to blame, check for broken lead wires, a

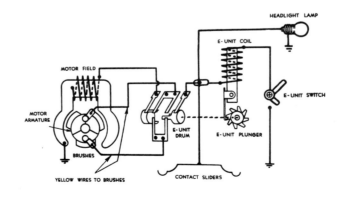

This schematic wiring diagram of a typical Lionel locomotive shows the universal motor, E-unit reversing mechanism, and headlight.

burned-out field coil, or brushes that aren't making contact with the commutator.

A noisy, sluggish, erratic, or hot-running motor suggests the brushes are sticking. To fix this problem, start by carefully removing the brush plate, brushes, and springs (don't let them jump out!). Visually inspect the brush plate for warpage; replace a badly warped plate, as it's almost impossible to straighten those old fiberboard assemblies without breaking them. Next, check for brush binding. Brushes should fit snugly within their brush wells, but their free in-and-out movement as they ride the commutator face must not be inhibited by dirt or anything else.

Clean the insides of the brush wells with TV Tuner Cleaner or solvent on a swab. Soak the brushes and springs in solvent until all the black residue has dissolved and they shine. If the brushes have worn into a lopsided angle, use emery paper or a fine file to square them. Replace the brushes if they are very short, and replace the brush springs if they have collapsed or lost their resiliency. Trying to bend or stretch them is a temporary solution at best.

In extreme cases, where the commutator surface is severely worn or pitted or has circular grooves cut into it, you must do more than routine cleaning with solvents. Lightly dress the commutator face with fine emery paper until you've removed all evidence of grooving and pitting. You should see no black rings or marks, only a clean copper surface. Most commutators have thick enough pole pieces to withstand this operation several times. Be careful not to wear away the coil wires in the process.

If you suspect there's something wrong with the armature, test it for short circuits and opening windings with a simple continuity tester or, better still, a volt-ohm-milliammeter. When doing these tests, either remove the brush plate entirely or get it out of the way to avoid any contact with the commutator. There should be no continuity between the armature shaft and any of the commutator segments. If the shaft has shorted against one or more of these segments, you need to consider rewinding or replacing the armature. As I've said before, coil winding is an advanced skill far beyond the technical scope of this book.

There should be continuity among the three segments of the commutator face. If there is a break in the continuity and an open segment results, replacement or rewinding may be indicated. However, sometimes the end of one of the coil wires simply may have broken away from its anchor on the commutator face and can be re-attached. If the loose wire is long enough, solder it back into position. Be sure to strip away the enamel from the section you intend to solder.

Worn-out armature bearings can allow the armature to rub against the field as it spins. You can detect this noisy condition by examining the armature for shiny wear spots along the edges of its plates. On some motors, these bearings are accessible and replaceable. If they aren't, consider the situation to be terminal. Offer a eulogy and either bury the motor or give it to a collector. Those guys never run their trains anyway!

Thermostatic Switches

Lionel used thermostatic switches to make lights blink, bells ring, and trains stop or start automatically long before the dawn of the electronic age. At the heart of the technology was a bimetallic strip, with a coil of high resistance nichrome wire wrapped around it. The nichrome coil, which was insulated from the bimetallic strip by a thin layer of asbestos (gasp!), acted as a miniature heating element while an electrical current was sent through it. When heated, the strip, by definition two dissimilar metals connected together at both ends, would bend because the different metals didn't expand at the same rate. As the strip bent, it would either make or break its electrical connection with a fixed contact. Once the strip had cooled, it returned to its normal, rest position.

Engineers at Lionel had two basic applications for thermostatic switches. One was to stop trains for a brief time at block signals, semaphores, or stations. The other was to control accessories that required intermittent action, such as flashing, ringing, or pumping

The switches used in the first of these applications had contacts that normally were open. They were connected to an insulated block of track that stopped the train at an appropriate place each time. When the thermostatic switch heated up, the contacts closed and fed power into the insulated

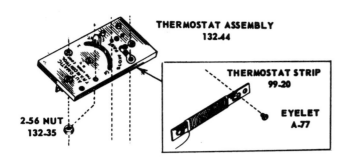 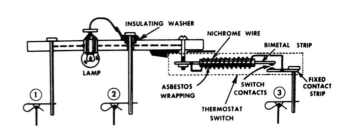

This illustration (left) and wiring diagram (right) show how a thermostatic switch is used on a 132 illuminated passenger station.

block long enough for the train to start up and leave it. Operators could use an adjustment lever on the signal or inside the station to control the duration of the stop interval or, if desired, to eliminate it altogether.

The earliest applications of this technology used a circuit that was completed through an insulated running-rail track section or a pressure contactor to heat the resistance coil. Designers later modified the circuit to a more sophisticated one that used the locomotive motor to accomplish the same thing. Because of the resistance of the nichrome wire, the current flowing through it was too low to operate the engine, yet high enough to heat the wire and bend the bimetallic strip.

A number of prewar and postwar accessories used this type of thermostatic switch. They included the 115, 116, 132, 136, and 137 stations, along with the 78 and 99 block signals, 82 semaphore, and 253 block control signal.

The thermostatic switches used in the second application had contacts that normally were closed. Because an intermittent action was required, the same circuit that operated the accessory also fed the coil in the switch. When the coil heated up, the contacts opened. As the switch cooled, contact was restored momentarily and the cycle repeated itself.

Accessories that used thermostatic switches to generate intermittent action were the prewar 79 flashing highway signal, 83 traffic and crossing signal, and 87 railroad crossing signal. During the postwar years, engineers relied on these switches to create unique activity on the 193 industrial water tower, 410 billboard blinker, and 455 oil derrick and pump. Similar switches also controlled the ringing bells in the tenders of ten different Lionel steam switch engines.

If you have an accessory whose thermostatic switch doesn't function, check for a burned-out or broken nichrome wire. This wire tends to burn or break off near the rivets at the ends of the bimetallic strip. Often you can unwind just enough wire from the coil to reattach it. If not, you can obtain replacement wire from some dealers and parts suppliers. Be sure you use the right kind and have the same

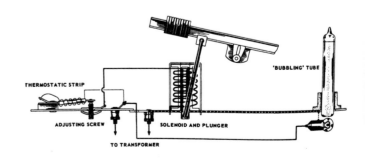

A thermostatic switch is used to energize the solenoid that drives the pump arm on a 455 oil derrick.

number of windings as were on the coil originally.

Poorly functioning switches may be caused by dirty or pitted contacts. Clean them with TV Tuner Cleaner or mineral spirits. File pitted contact surfaces slightly until they're smooth. As a final note, you can adjust the time interval to some extent by carefully bending the fixed contacts in either direction.

AFTERWORD

We've gone through all the preliminaries and basics, from transformers and track to rolling stock and accessories, from layout construction to wiring. We even took a look at the mechanical and electrical aspects of classic toy train technology. I hope this general overview has interested you enough to get you started in (or hooked on) the toy train hobby.

Understanding how and why the trains work is essential unless you're going to be a collector and just line up your trains on shelves and gaze at them. That's a shame because they were made to run. Most will with just a little help and some primary-level maintenance.

I realize that we have been dealing with trains that suffered mainly from neglect and long storage. We assumed that they were complete and in good condition otherwise. That's not always the case in the real world. Things get broken or quit working before they are packed away for the last time; that's often the reason they were packed away. I also know how frustrating that can be. I've been repairing, refurbishing, and restoring trains for a long time. That's where the hobby has led me.

I've run trains until I got dizzy and collected them until the floor sagged. Now, my greatest pleasure comes from recycling them. To me, making them look and run like new again is both a kick and a challenge. With all the replacement parts on the market, it is one heck of a lot easier than it used to be. In the old days, we were lucky to find enough good parts to make one usable piece out of two beaters. Sometimes we got two from three, but that was rare. We certainly couldn't make two from two, because there just weren't any parts available. That's all changed. Some dealers specialize in nothing but spare parts. You can even buy paints in the correct colors and replacement lettering that matches the original.

Since 1990, my repair projects have appeared

as a series of articles in *Classic Toy Trains* magazine. I've taken apart sick trains and accessories, examined their innards, and diagnosed their maladies. Then I made them whole again. Readers liked my approach, so my next book will get into these more advanced service and repair techniques for individual trains and accessories. I may look at some sophisticated track wiring projects, though Peter Riddle's books on wiring Lionel trains have that waterfront well covered.

I will, however, delve into restoration work in depth and promise to share my experiences in hopes of enhancing your operation and collection. There's nothing you can't master if the desire is in you. If I can do it, you certainly can.

That will be in the next book. Look for it in another year or so. In the meantime, here are some fine books to keep you busy and make the hobby enjoyable. All of them should be available from your local hobby retailer or you can order any or all of them direct from Kalmbach Publishing Co., 21027 Crossroads Circle, Waukesha, WI 53187-1612; 1-800-533-6644.

Suggested Readings About Toy Trains

I. General Readings

Grams, John. *Beginner's Guide to Toy Train Collecting and Operating*. A complete introduction to collecting, maintaining, and operating toy trains. Teaches novices how to start and add to a collection, determine value and price, develop specialties, and build a layout.

Kelly, Jim. *Fun with Electric Trains*. Cuts through complicated wiring and scenery to answer questions about keeping trains on the track and running. Shows how to build five basic yet attractive layouts.

Model Railroader magazine. *The ABC's of Model Railroading*. Ideal for beginners, this book is a complete primer on basic tips and techniques that is simple and easy to follow. Explains track, wiring, tools, benchwork, structures, and more. From the pages of *Model Railroader*, it is geared to the scale modeler, but much can be applied to toy train layouts as well.

Riddle, Peter. *Trains from Grandfather's Attic*. An informative layout book about pre–World War II trains. Discusses layout purpose and design, construction, and operation. Beautifully restored antique locomotives, rolling stock, and accessories.

II. History of Toy Trains

Greenberg Books has put out more than fifty authoritative reference books about the history of American toy trains. The output of the major and a number of the minor toy train producers has been cataloged, inventoried, categorized, and dissected in the series, which is organized by manufacturer and era. You'll find just about everything that you want to know about virtually every train and train-related item made since the beginning of this century: Lionel, American Flyer, Marx, Ives, Hafner, Kusan, and Dorfan, among others, have been covered.

III. Model Railroad Layouts Using Toy Trains

Classic Toy Trains magazine. *Toy Train Layout Tour*. A tour of more than a dozen of America's most outstanding toy train layouts, originally featured in the pages of *Classic Toy Trains* magazine. Action-packed layouts show the fun of modeling with Lionel and American Flyer trains. This book is highly informative and inspirational, and is sure to delight toy train fans of all ages.

Lesser, Josef and Peter Youngblood. *Realistic Railroading with Toy Trains*. The blending of toy trains and scale modeling is called "hi-rail modeling." It is fast becoming the direction in which toy train operators are moving. Lesser and Youngblood document the building of the JL/ATSF, a hi-rail O gauge layout, and provide the step-by-step information needed to build one of your own.

IV. Repair and Operating Guides

Greenberg, Bruce C. *Greenberg's Repair and Operating Manual for Lionel Trains, 1945–1969*. More than 700 pages of the most useful schematics and exploded diagrams, along with detailed repair instructions and diagnostic advice. Covers trains made between 1945 and 1969, but many of the theories and techniques are applicable to trains made before and since. Probably not for the novice.

Riddle, Peter. *Tips and Tricks for Toy Train Operators*. More than a hundred ideas for improving the appearance and operation of toy train layouts. Illustrated techniques, easy-to-follow diagrams, detailed photos, and clear and concise text. For novices and experts alike.

V. Scenery and Structures

Frary, Dave. *Realistic Scenery for Toy Train Layouts*. Toy train operators have come to appreciate the dramatic impact that realistic scenery can add to their layouts. This how-to book introduces the basic tools of scenery building, then walks readers through several scenery projects using proven techniques. Shows how easy it is to add detail and realism to even the simplest layout.

Frary, Dave. *222 Tips for Building Model Railroad Structures*. Practical advice and expert opinions. Tips for plastic, wood, plaster, paper, and metal structures. Includes detailing and weathering.

Model Railroader magazine. *Scenery Tips and Techniques*. A collection of outstanding scenery articles makes up this guide to easy, inexpensive, and imaginative scenic detailing that uses time-tested methods and updated techniques. For all scales and gauges, listed by topic and indexed.

VI. Track Planning, Layout Construction, and Wiring

Lang, Cliff. *Layout Plans for Lionel Trains*. A compilation of more than 100 plans to assist in designing layouts, from *Model Builder* magazine. Includes a detailed description of how to design and build the compact 4 x 8-foot layout described in the text.

Riddle, Peter. *Greenberg's Wiring Your Lionel Layout*. Volume 1: *A Primer For Lionel Train Enthusiasts* and Volume 2: *Intermediate Techniques* are just what readers of this book need to progress with their understanding of Lionel's electrical technology. Each features easy-to-read text and step-by-step instructions on completing tested and useful projects.

Trzoniec, Stanley. *How to Build Your First Lionel Layout*. The novice Lionel enthusiast, ready to build that first layout, will find this book indispensable. Detailed photos and easy-to-follow instructions on each phase of layout construction: track planning, benchwork, wiring, and scenery techniques. Handy section on troubleshooting and maintenance.

Westcott, Linn. *How to Build Model Railroad Benchwork*. The newly revised edition of this classic work includes new tools, materials, and techniques that make benchwork construction easier than ever before. Illustrated step-by-step instructions show how to assemble basic framework for layouts of any size, shape, or gauge. Special supports for backdrops, helixes, turntables, and more have been included.